ROUTLEDGE LIBRARY EDITIONS: CHINESE LITERATURE AND ARTS

Volume 13

FIFTY SONGS FROM THE YÜAN

FIFTY SONGS FROM THE YÜAN

Poetry of 13th Century China

Translated by
RICHARD F. S. YANG and
CHARLES R. METZGER

LONDON AND NEW YORK

First published in 1967 by George Allen & Unwin Ltd

This edition first published in 2022
by Routledge
4 Park Square, Milton Park, Abingdon, Oxon OX14 4RN

and by Routledge
605 Third Avenue, New York, NY 10158

Routledge is an imprint of the Taylor & Francis Group, an informa business

© 1967 UNESCO

All rights reserved. No part of this book may be reprinted or reproduced or utilised in any form or by any electronic, mechanical, or other means, now known or hereafter invented, including photocopying and recording, or in any information storage or retrieval system, without permission in writing from the publishers.

Trademark notice: Product or corporate names may be trademarks or registered trademarks, and are used only for identification and explanation without intent to infringe.

British Library Cataloguing in Publication Data
A catalogue record for this book is available from the British Library

ISBN: 978-0-367-11183-0 (Set)
ISBN: 978-1-032-24883-7 (Volume 13) (hbk)
ISBN: 978-1-032-24885-1 (Volume 13) (pbk)
ISBN: 978-1-003-28055-2 (Volume 13) (ebk)

DOI: 10.4324/9781003280552

Publisher's Note
The publisher has gone to great lengths to ensure the quality of this reprint but points out that some imperfections in the original copies may be apparent.

Disclaimer
The publisher has made every effort to trace copyright holders and would welcome correspondence from those they have been unable to trace.

FIFTY SONGS FROM THE YÜAN

POETRY OF 13th CENTURY CHINA

―――――

TRANSLATED, WITH INTRODUCTION, APPENDICES
AND NOTES BY
RICHARD F. S. YANG AND CHARLES R. METZGER

London
GEORGE ALLEN & UNWIN LTD
RUSKIN HOUSE   MUSEUM STREET

FIRST PUBLISHED IN 1967

*This book is copyright under the Berne Convention.
A part from any fair dealing for the purposes of private
study, research, criticism or review, as permitted under
the Copyright Act, 1956, no portion may be
reproduced by any process without written permission.
Enquiries should be addressed to the publishers.*

© UNESCO 1967

PRINTED IN GREAT BRITAIN
in 11 point Old Style
BY UNWIN BROTHERS LTD
WOKING AND LONDON

ACKNOWLEDGEMENT

During the more than two and one half years that we have been working on this project we have become indebted for their assistance to a number of benefactors. We wish to acknowledge this indebtedness, and for that reason dedicate this small volume, to the following persons and institutions: Professor Cheng Ch'ien of the University of Taiwan who selected the *ch'ü* that we have translated and provided material for the biographical sketches of known authors, to the University of Southern California, for among other things its Faculty Research and Assistance Grants to the two of us, to Professor William H. Werkmeister, Director of the School of Philosophy, who in his capacity as editor of *The Personalist* accepted for publication the first seven of our *ch'ü* and has granted us permission to reprint them in this volume, to Mrs Frances Demmon, Mrs Marie Buboltz, and Miss Cheryl Erskine, for typing the manuscript several times, to Mr Daniel L. Milton for his encouragement, advice, and assistance in preparing the final manuscript and for seeing it through the press, and to our wives, Myrtle and Carol, who are exemplary cooks, mothers, wives, and critics.
Los Angeles, 1965

Richard Fu-Sen Yang
Charles R. Metzger

CONTENTS

INTRODUCTION	*page* 11
FIFTY SONGS FROM THE YÜAN	
giving, for each poem:	
a The final English poetic translation	
b The original Chinese text	19
Appendices to the Fifty Poems:	
giving, for each poem:	
a The transliterated Chinese text	
b A word-by-word translation	
c A first-draft translation	
d Notes (where required)	85
Remarks on the Transliterated and Word-by-Word Texts	139
Biographical Sketches of the Poets	143
Index of Poets	147
Index of English Titles	148
Index of First Lines	150

INTRODUCTION

The major forms of Chinese poetry written between the end of the Chou dynasty and the period after the Yüan dynasty, when opera became predominant, have been associated by literary historians with the names of the intervening dynasties themselves. Thus historians refer to the *fu* form of the Han dynasty, the *shih* of the T'ang, the *tz'u* of Sung, and the *ch'ü* of Yüan. Very little poetry of the Yüan dynasty has been translated into English.

The following poems, written during the Yüan dynasty (chiefly in the thirteenth century under Mongol rule), demonstrate the *ch'ü* or song form of poetry dominant in that period. The *ch'ü* was a popular form of poetry, pastoral in the sense that it was written by educated poets in vernacular rather than in classical Chinese. Each poem was written to be sung to an already popular tune.*

The Yüan was not entirely a happy time for Chinese intellectuals. Under Mongol rule the civil service examinations, relatively undisturbed by the rulers of previous dynasties, were abolished. Held at local, state, and imperial levels, these examinations had been designed to screen candidates for public office and to insure their competency. Such examinations, including as they did a section which required each candidate to compose a poem upon a given topic and according to a stipulated rhyme scheme and pattern of syllable count, tended to favour candidates with literary talent. Needless to say, civil service candidates from rich and powerful families (families that hired tutors for their sons and sent them to schools) were certain of instruction in verse-writing.

* As suggested in the brief biographical sketches which we have presented, several of the poets of *ch'ü* also wrote operatic drama. In China, as elsewhere, the drama and the song combined quite naturally (with the addition of recitative) to produce opera, in which the *ch'ü*, or some versions of *ch'ü*, often functioned as arias.

Under Mongol rule the civil service examinations, abolished at the outset, were reinstated only shortly before the end of Mongol dominion. Under Mongol rule literary talent was not particularly encouraged or rewarded. (Mongols ironically referred to the Chinese as *man-tzu*, or barbarians.) However, literary talent, once developed, tends to exercise itself whether encouraged to do so or not. When officially discouraged, it often turns its attention to lyric composition, such composition frequently suggesting by indirection criticism of the regime. Intelligent and semi-aristocratic Chinese, having seen better times and having been trained to write poetry, tended often in their poetry to celebrate the past, to ignore or to draw direct attention away from current affairs. The *ch'ü* presented here were written mostly by North Chinese, over whom Mongol dominion was most secure. Accordingly these *ch'ü* bear an unmistakably Taoist caste, rejecting 'merit and fame', i.e. connection with the ruling families: and rejecting as well the values associated with these abstractions, 'merit and fame', and with royal connection.

The poets who originally composed these *ch'ü*—possibly because they had lost their courtly audience (since such audience during the Yüan was composed primarily of Mongols with an admixture of Moslems, Tartars, and Koreans)—chose to write in what was probably the more profitable vernacular, rather than in classical Chinese. Identifying, perhaps realistically, with the lesser classes that they had suddenly joined, they may have chosen to exercise their aristocratic talents in vernacular Chinese for that reason alone. They may have chosen, however, to use vernacular Chinese rather than classical Chinese for reasons similar to those of Dante, Chaucer, and other near-contemporaries in far distant lands, living there under quite different circumstances,—for the reason that vernacular Chinese, like the vernacular Italian and the vernacular English, was emerging into linguistic dominance. The poets of *ch'ü* may have chosen to write in vernacular Chinese and to ally their poetry with popular songs for semi-propagandistic reasons: to solicit support from uneducated persons, who though they might not be able to read, could yet listen.

The fact that some of the authors of *ch'ü* were 'assimilated' Moslems may suggest a number of things: that the popularity of the *ch'ü* indicated which way the wind was beginning to blow, that the topics treated were universal, that sensitive immigrants, whether literate in their own languages or not, tend to pick up first the vernacular language of their adopted country.

In form the *ch'ü* are characterized by a high incidence of rhyme, with all or all but a few of the lines ending in the same rhyme. The individual *ch'ü* (or *hsiao-ling*), as well as the 'chains' of *ch'ü* (or *t'ao-shu*), are also identified by a fairly strict syllable count. Slightly longer, for the most part, than the later Japanese *tanka*, the individual *ch'ü* of Yüan are often characterized by the same sharp imagery and seasonal references. The last three 'poems' in this collection are actually 'chains' of *ch'ü* (or *t'ao-shu*) which anticipate their Japanese counterpart, the *renga* (or 'chains' of *tanka*), just as, similarly, the individual *ch'ü* anticipate the more rigid *tanka* and its offshoot the *haiku*.

In attempting to translate into modern English the principal forms of thirteenth-century *ch'ü*, i.e. the *hsiao-ling*, or single song set to a single tune (including occasionally pairs of *ch'ü* set to the same tune and also single *ch'ü* set to two tunes intended to be sung in harmony), and in attempting to translate the song chains (the *t'ao-shu*) composed of several *hsiao-ling*, involving varieties in combination of tunes and syllable counts, we as translators have had to make a number of crucial decisions and have had to accept in accordance with our decisions certain limitations. On this account, and in view of the somewhat different kinds of readers to whom we present this work, we have arranged our offering in its present form.

Readers in translation of the more familiar *haiku* and *tanka* are acquainted with the custom of arranging such poetic translations according to the four seasons. We have chosen not to arrange our translations in this manner for three reasons: (1) These are not Japanese poems in translation, but Chinese poems. (2) Even if the *ch'ü* were grossly similar to the *tanka* and *haiku*, which usually they are not, our own experience is that five or six poems addressed to the same season, e.g. Spring, or to the same topic, e.g. love, lead the reader quickly to become surfeited with Spring, and even with love as a topic.

(3) Our selection of topics is too varied: the four seasons are inadequate to provide a defensible scheme of presentation. Accordingly we have mixed the seasons, the topics, the authors, to provide what we consider to be a fair cross-section of *ch'ü*.

We have, in support of our presentation, provided appendices, footnotes, biographical sketches (when available) to enable those readers who care (including students of Chinese language and literature) to search out all the translations here presented of poems by any single known writer,* and to check also and to evaluate our translations and our methods.

From some of our colleagues, translators of *haiku*, *tanka*, and *renga*, we have adopted the following procedures. We have chosen to hold as faithfully as possible to syllable count, to imagery, to tone, and to the sense of each poem since we consider these indispensable to the proper translation of *ch'ü*. Faithfulness to rhyme-scheme appears to us unrewardingly awkward, given the different natures of the English and Chinese languages. The responsibility of rhyming with the same endings six or seven succeeding lines of English verse (as is readily possible in Chinese) is one which, as translators, we feel we cannot accept without wrenching our translations: without slighting the other, to us, more important responsibilities that we have already accepted. Thus like many translators of the shorter and in a sense easier *haiku*, we have chosen to dispense with rhyme, even though rhyme is a major feature of *ch'ü*, as well as of *haiku* and *tanka*.

Having chosen, along with some of our fellow translators of *haiku* and *tanka*, to hold to syllable count, imagery, and tone, we have had to pay the same price as our colleagues for doing so. In translating Chinese or Japanese into English, in working from characters to romanic transcription, in working from romanized transliterations to English verse, from a language in which a single character may amount to either a word, a phrase, or even an entire period in the other language and vice versa, we have had to face serious problems. One character, one syllable, in Chinese, may require an entire predication to render it into English. Every time a Chinese general, an official, or a poet is named, the English translator loses two or more precious

* See author indices.

syllables. In a fairly complex poem containing only fifty syllables, this loss can be heart-rending.

Given the decisions we have made regarding the problems posed by our attempts to translate poetry from a non-Indo-European language into English verse, there is likely to have accrued to our production a considerable amount of loss and hopefully some of gain, if not gain in point of information, at least in point of tone.

For Western readers who are interested primarily in examining the final results of our endeavour, interested in reading what amounts to a new form of English poetry (which, as translators, we have had to invent),* interested in learning something about what it must have been like to live as displaced but not usually exiled members of the Chinese intelligentsia during the Yüan dynasty, we have presented in the first section of this edition our final product: English poetic translations of fifty songs or *ch'ü* from the Yüan. For students of Chinese poetry we have also presented on the same page, or in the case of longer poems on the opposite page, the original poems.

In this first section we have listed in connection with each poem, the author's name, when known, the title of each poem, when known, (when a poem is untitled we have added what we consider to be an appropriate 'English' title), the tune or tunes to which each poem was intended to be sung (the scores using the traditional Chinese musical scale have to our knowledge, been unrecorded or lost†), the syllable count for each original poem, and our present English translation along with the original poem. We have tried, in so far as possible, to remain faithful to the sense, the tone, the syllable count, of each poem, capitalizing as much as we have thought appropriate upon the resources of English versification: alliteration, imagery, enjambment, caesura, rhythm, etc.

In the appendices to each poem, we have presented our

---

* Ezra Pound for example appears not to have kept entirely faithful to syllable count, even though his translations, done in collaboration with a Korean scholar well-versed in Chinese literature, are truly works of genius.

† Even as this volume was going to press, I discovered at the Academia Sinica in Taipei that most of the tunes are known. We hope eventually to have these printed in a companion volume. R.F.S.Y.

working copy, as well as explanatory notes, by way of indicating our method of translation and by way of enabling students of Chinese literature to judge the validity of our work, and by way also of providing the English speaking reader with explanatory notes in cases where these seem advisable.

Our method of translation has involved, as the appendices demonstrate, Professor Yang's transliteration first of each original poem, using the standard Wade-Giles system of transliteration, into romanic script. The non-Chinese scholar or reader can, accordingly, by consulting our brief description of the Wade-Giles system of romanic transliteration, get some idea of how the original poems actually would have sounded (as spoken, of course, rather than sung).

For convenience to the student, or to the scholar, or to the English-speaking reader, we have provided in addition to various indices of titles, authors, first lines, etc., brief biographies of the poets of *ch'ü*, about whom information is available.

Although in the main the poems as translated are self-explanatory, a few hints may be of help to some readers. The willow often suggests the figure of a slim young woman. The crane is a symbol of longevity: 'May you live as long as a crane', is a nice thing to say to a friend. In addition to the crane, the pine tree and the tortoise also suggest longevity. On occasion, references to the tortoise suggest the practice of divination by interpreting the significance of the markings on a tortoise shell as a way of telling fortune. Although lotus flowers are beautiful and to be appreciated accordingly, their seeds provide an edible delicacy, and persons plucking lotus may have gastronomical as well as aesthetic motives.

Ducks, particularly if they are Mandarin ducks, suggest well and permanently married couples, as do the phoenix which always fly in pairs. Swallows and orioles generally suggest Spring. The cuckoo in Chinese poetry does not, as in Western tradition, suggest cuckoldry, but rather, sad, springtime love. More nearly like the European nightingale, the cuckoo suggests sadness, longing, even death from unrequited love. When sufficiently distraught, the cuckoo sings until it bleeds to death from its bill. The owl, reputed in Chinese poetic tradition to be unable to build its own nest, occupies, after the manner of the cuckoo in Western tradition, the nests of other birds.

The colour green in reference to a thing, i.e. 'green smoke', 'green horse', generally suggests freshness, youth, and vigour. Western winds indicate the approach of autumn.

A fair amount of wine appears to have been drunk during the Yüan, possibly for the perfectly good reason that in a complex society where its citizens were under great pressure (particularly those formerly of high rank), some forms of escape were virtually indispensable, such as painting, poetry, travel, female company, drink. The wine consumed was probably made from rice, possibly also from plums and other fruits. Occasionally the Chinese minor official of the Yüan, like his modern Western counterpart, over-imbibed. Men grew old during the Yüan, as at any other time, and were sad about it, often taking to their cups. Courtesans and wives had also occasion to be sad, to weep, even take to drink. Similarly, good friends became sad when forced to part. Customarily such friends commemorated their parting with drink—the better the friendship, the more wine consumed. Wine was also used by Chinese poets, painters, philosophers, to induce inspiration. The drinking of wine for this purpose was considered to be particularly effective when undertaken in the company of a 'sing-song girl'. Sometimes confused with the courtesan or prostitute, the Chinese 'sing-song girl', counterpart to the Japanese *geisha*, was an intelligent, highly-trained, and relatively chaste professional companion and entertainer.

Warfare was as much a part of normal life during the Yüan as it has been since. Poems concerning victories, defeats, poems expressing nostalgic reminiscences of gain or loss, celebrate these fierce facts of life.

Twig-breaking suggests some kind of formal, ceremonial expression of respect or congratulation. To break off a twig from a willow or a cinnamon and give it to a person is the Chinese equivalent of awarding the laurel or palm in Western culture. The cinnamon-breaking ceremony is particularly significant. A freshly broken cinnamon twig was presented usually by the Empress to the candidate for entrance into palace service who had received the highest score in civil-service examinations leading to the highest governmental offices, those connected with serving the Imperial Court.

The breaking of a willow branch in these and other Chinese poems always suggests departure usually performed at a so-called 'long pavilion' specially erected for that purpose outside a city wall.

I

Author: Kuan Han-ch'ing
Title: 'Sad Parting'
Tune: 'Four Pieces of Jade'
Syllable count: 3, 3, 7, 7, 3, 3, 3

    I cannot
    Bear a love
    Cut off. My sleeve removes the
    Willow's snow. Winding fades the
    Stream beyond
    My hill-stopped
    Lover's view.

一、四塊玉　　　　關漢卿
　　　別　情
　自送別
　心難捨
　一點相思幾時絕
　憑欄袖拂楊花雪
　溪又斜
　山又遮
　人去也

Author: Po P'u
Title: 'Drink Song'
Tune: 'Parasitic Grass'
Syllable count: 6, 6, 7, 7, 7, 8, 8

Drink deep. What matters? Who
Cares, when drunk, for merit
Or for fame! Spirits blind times
Of strife. Rainbows sink beyond
Oceans. Kings err, but T'ao Ch'ien
Is right. All those who read these times
Know Ch'ü Yüan's wrong, and T'ao Ch'ien's right.

二. 寄生草　　　白樸
　　　勸飲
長醉後方何礙
不醒時有甚思
糟醃兩個功名字
醅淹千古興亡事
麴埋萬丈虹霓志
不達時皆笑屈原非
但知音盡說陶潛是

Author: Po P'u
Title: 'Career Song'
Tune: 'Celebration in Tung-yüan,
Syllable count: 3, 3, 7, 7, 7, 7, 5, 5

Tear-spent grass,
Cheerful blooms,
Urge retirement now in time:
Still is Lu Chia's voice, lost Tzu
Ya's advice. Brave Chang Hua is
Dead. A thousand years of work
For right, count as one
Quiet chat by night.

三．慶東原　　　白　樸

草花
憂笑
忘含
勸君聞早冠宜掛
那裡也能言陸賈賣
那裡也良謀子牙
那裡也豪氣張華
千古是非心
一夕漁樵話

Author: Po P'u
Title: 'Old Fisherman's Song'
Tune: 'Heavily Drunk in the East Wind'
Syllable count: 7, 7, 5, 5, 7, 7, 7

Fishing willowed stream, seining
By sandy beach, timeless as
His friends: proud, not fierce,
Unlettered still, he,
Like stately wading crane, and,
Swooping sandy gull, lives on,
More venerably than dukes.

四. 沉醉東風　　　　白樸
　　　　漁父詞
黃蘆岸白蘋渡口
綠楊堤紅蓼灘頭
雖無刎頸交
却有忘機友
點秋江白鷺沙鷗
傲殺人間萬戶侯
不識字煙波釣叟

5

Author: Yang Kuo
Title: 'Lotus Song, I'
Tune: 'Little Red Peach'
Syllable count: 7, 5, 7, 3, 7, 4, 4, 5

Sing! Pick lotus! Let orchid
Sampans slide. Forget
Love, now passed! From the tower
After night
Of lonesome sadness, sing—but
Not the Southern
Songs of kings. Tears
For them dry quickly.

五 小桃紅　　　楊果
　　採蓮歌㈠
採蓮人和採蓮歌
柳外蘭舟過
不管鴛鴦夢鷖破
夜如何
有人獨上江樓臥
傷心莫唱
南朝舊曲
司馬淚痕多

6

'Lotus Song, II'

Lotus picking, I come late.
The wind sings varied
Songs of tears. Mimosas droop
And you're not
Here. The evening's cold! Ducks
And cranes now fail
To flock as they
Once did, together.

六．小桃紅　　　楊果
　　採蓮歌㈡
採蓮湖上棹船迴
風約湘裙翠
一曲琵琶數行淚
望君歸
芙蓉開盡無消息
晚涼多少
紅鴛白鷺
何處不雙飛

7

Author: Hu Chih-yü
Title: 'Autumnal Song'
Tune: 'One Half'
Syllable count: 7, 7, 7, 3, 8

    Lotus leaves now fade—even as
Chrysanthemums grow yellow.
Maple leaves turn red, as trunks of
Tungs grow green.
Western winds bring Autumn with frost.

七. 一半兒　　　　胡祗遹
　　四季：秋

荷盤減翠菊花黃
楓葉飄紅梧幹蒼
鴛被不禁昨夜涼
釀秋光
一半兒西風一半兒霜

8

Author: Hu Chih-yü
Title: 'Spring Song'
Tune: 'One Half'
Syllable count: 7, 7, 7, 3, 8

With light shirt and short hat I
Ride a seven scented cart. These
Scents are like pictures. But what
Makes gay flowers
Droop? Wind and rain both share the guilt!

八 · 一半兒　　　　胡祗遹
　　四季：春
輕衫短帽七香車
九十春光如畫圖
明日落紅誰是主
漫躊躇
一半兒因風一半兒雨

Author: Yao Sui
Title: 'Winter Song'
Tune: 'Singing Loud When Drunk'
Syllable count: 6, 6, 7, 6

Ten years of song 'neath moons
Of Yen have turned my hair
To frost. As perch return to
Seas, I greet evening thoughts.

九．醉高歌　　姚燧
　　感懷
十年燕月歌聲
幾點吳霜鬢影
西風吹起鱸魚興
已在桑榆暮景

Author: Yao Sui
Title: 'Old Scholar's Spring Song'
Tune: 'Happy With the Coming of Spring'
Syllable count: 7, 7, 7, 3, 5

My brush fixes time with ink.
Children exceed my verse. When
Asked, I say: 'Broad seas are rich;
Unconcerned
Are fish with figures.'

十 喜春來　　　　姚 燧

筆頭風月時時過
眼底兒曹漸漸多
有人問我事如何
人海闊
無日不風波

11

Author: Ma Chih-yüan
Title: 'Meditation in Autumn'
Tune: 'The Sky is so Pure'
Syllable count: 6, 6, 6, 4, 6

Dry vine, tree, evening crow:
Lone hut, quick stream, small bridge,
Old road, west wind, lean horse.
Sunset suggests
To this old man, his fate!

Author: Chang Yang-hao
Title: 'Sad Question'
Tune: 'Happiness to the Wide World'
Syllable count: 3, 3, 4, 4, 3, 3, 4, 5, 7, 4, 4, 4

Who fathoms
Li-sao: its
Meaning? Heaven
Knows! Gone to please
The fish of
Hsiang, this man
Who misbehaved,
Singing drunk mid green
Mountains, sampled pleasure to
Its end, and was
Dismissed by his
Sober princes.

十二. 普天樂　　　張養浩

楚離騷　　空快活了
誰能解　　湘江魚蝦蟹
就中之意　這先生暢好是胡來
日月明白　怎如向青山影裡
恨尚存　　狂歌痛飲
人何在　　其樂無涯

Author: Chang Yang-hao
Title: 'Consolatory Thought'
Tune: 'Audience with the King'
Syllable count: 2, 2, 6, 7, 5, 4, 4, 5, 2, 2, 6

    Impeached
    I now
    Retire. Ambition's vain
    When rowdy, stupid, gross!
    Today, while wandering
    Woods, I knew that
    Thirty years can
    Buy reward, when trees
    Can thus
    Suggest,
    Pleasure in retirement.

Author: Anonymous
Title: 'Grave Heroes'
Tune: 'Red Embroidered Shoes'
Syllable count: 7, 7, 7, 5, 5, 6

    King Pa was brave; he saved his
    Face. Kao-tsu killed a white snake.
    Moonlight now bathes Kao-tsu's tomb.
    Clouds cover Ch'u's shrine.
    Are there any more
    Such heroes left to us?

十四. 紅繡鞋　　　　　無名

楚霸王休誇勇烈
漢高祖莫說豪傑
一個舉鼎拔山一個斬白蛇
漢陵殘月照
楚廟暮雲遮
二英雄何去也

Author: Anonymous
Title: 'Old Soldier's Song'
Tune: 'Parasitic Grass'
Syllable count: 3, 3, 8, 8, 8, 7, 7

Fighting with
Great skill, but
Pressing too hard at Red Bluff, he
Fell into Chou-lang's river trap.
With this one man died the skills of
Three. Waiting for posterity
To judge him—let us drink wine!

十五．寄生草　　　無名

爭閒氣
使見識
赤壁山正中周郎計
烏江岸枉使重瞳力
馬嵬坡空灑明皇淚
前人勳業後人看
不如今朝醉了明朝醉

Author: Chang Yang-hao
Title: 'A New Life'
Tune: 'The Twelfth Month' with 'The Song of the People of Yao'
Syllable count: 7, 7, 7, 7, 7, 7, 7, 7, 7, 7, 5

Fled from fierce merit and fame,
I view this fair land of flowers
And moons. Five hundred acres—rain
Ploughed, smoke tilled! Without fear I
Sleep till dawn. Only here do
I watch the chickens and dogs
of Hsieh-ch'uan enjoy their hours
Of peaceful livelihood. From
My small house amidst Hemp and
Mulberry I can see now
At last, with pleasure, green smoke
Rising toward the sky.

十六．十二月帶堯民歌　　張養浩

從跳出功名火坑
來到這花月蓬瀛
守着這良田數頃
看一會雨種烟耕
到大來心頭不驚
每日家直睡到天明
見斜川雞犬樂昇平
繞屋桑麻翠烟生
杖藜無處不堪行
滿目雲山畫難成
泉聲響時子細聽
轉覺柴門靜

Author: Kuan Yun-shih
Title: 'Written for Someone'
Tune: 'Wild Geese in Autumn Outside the Great Wall'
Syllable count: 8, 7, 7, 7, 5, 5, 3, 5

Despite west winds, come welcomed geese.
One thinks of the sad fates of
Past dynasties. Scribe the clean
Paper with sweet songs of sadness!
Genius fails my quick
Brush. Tired, today, I
Write only
Of mutual love.

十七. 塞鴻秋　　　貫雲石
　　　代人作
戰西風幾點賓鴻至
感起我南朝千古傷心事
展花箋欲寫幾句知心事
空交我停霜毫半晌無才思
往常得興時
一掃無瑕疵
今日個病厭厭
剛寫下兩個相思字

Author: Teng Yü-pin
Title: 'Leisure Living'
Tune: 'A Goose Falls' with 'Song of Victory'
Syllable count: 5, 5, 5, 5, 5, 5, 5, 5, 2, 5, 2, 5

    Sun and moon rotate.
    So move our lives and
    Dreams. Jade gates are far
    Distant. My fishing
    Beach counts seven miles.
    At dawn Chang-an draws
    Close. Sze-chuan's road
    Is hard. Stop! Think how
    A brave
    Hero is wasted!
    White are
    My starry temples.

十八．雁兒落帶得勝令　　鄧玉賓
　　　閒適

乾坤一轉丸　　　　曉日長安近
日月雙飛箭　　　　秋風蜀道難
浮生夢一場　　　　休干
世事雲千變　　　　誤殺英雄漢
萬里玉門關　　　　看看
七里釣魚灘　　　　星星雨鬢斑

Author: Pai Pen
Title: 'Pastoral Painter'
Tune: 'Parrot Song'
Syllable count: 7, 6, 7, 6, 7, 6, 7, 7

At Parrot Beach I live next
To illiterate fishers.
I sleep near their flat boats, all
Soundly, midst rain. Awake,
I see green mountains. In grass
Coat I wander. Painting
Escapes me, until I come
Back, freshed, to my wooden gate.

Author: Ma Chih-yüan
Title: 'Clearing Weather'
Tune: 'Fallen Plum Wind'
Syllable count: 3, 3, 7, 8, 7

As sun shines
Through morning
Rain, steaming mountains reveal
This verdant village. More green must
Now be added to my print.

二十. 落梅風　　　馬致遠
　　　山市晴嵐

花村外
草店西
曉霞明雨收天霽
四圍山一竿殘照裡
錦屏風又添鋪翠

Author: Yao Sui
Title: 'Song for the Seasons'
Tune: 'Plucking Cannot Harm It'
Syllable count: 3, 3, 7, 7, 7, 7

Grass grows green
As days grow
Long. Young folks frolic. It's spring!
Swallows swoop in the courtyard.
Ducks sleep serene on the sand.
Now is the time to plant flowers!

二十一．撥不斷　　　姚燧
　　　四時景

草萋萋
日遲遲
王孫士女春遊戲
宮殿風微燕雀飛
池塘沙暖鴛鴦睡
正值着養花天氣

Author: Hsüeh Ang-fu
Title: 'Old Man's Spring Song' I
Tune: 'Far is the Sky of Ch'u' with
       'The Pure River Flows'
Syllable count: 5, 5, 5, 5, 5, 5, 5, 7, 5, 5, 5, 7

    Past inebriates of
    Spring long in Summer
    To be drunk again,
    Surprised to find it
    Hard, while viewing streams
    Afresh with willows.
    Green willows just as
    Women, bear catkins.
    Who can collect these against
    The strong winds of age?
    Sorrows advance with
    Flow tides, and remain
    After ebb, leaving aged men.

二十二. 楚天遙帶清江引　　薛昂夫

　花開人正歡　花落春如醉
　春醉有時醒　人老歡難會
　一江春水流　萬點楊花墜
　誰道是楊花　點點離人淚
　回首有情風萬里
　渺渺天無際
　愁共海潮來　潮去愁難退
　更那堪晚來風又急

Author: Hsüeh Ang-fu
Title: 'Old Man's Spring Song' II
Tune: 'Far is the Sky of Ch'u' with
        'The Pure River Flows'
Syllable count: 5, 5, 5, 5, 5, 5, 5, 7, 5, 5, 5, 7

    Unable to retain
    Her, I let Spring go.
    She may return next
    Year, or not at all.
    Peach blossoms and jade
    Are rare as skies of
    Ch'u. Spring should be sad
    Since she dies every
    Year: since the sun sets daily
    Behind her mountains.
    Under the ferry her
    Waters flow. But where
    Do they come from, I ask you?

二十三. 楚天遙 帶 清江引 　　薛昂夫
　有意送春歸　無計留春住
　明年又着來　何似休歸去
　桃花也解愁　點點飄紅玉
　目斷楚天遙　不見春歸路
　春若有情春更苦
　暗裡韶光度
　　夕陽山外山　春水渡傍渡
　不知那答兒是春住處

Author: Li Chih-yüan
Title: 'Late Spring Song of a Wife'
Tune: 'Welcome to the Immortal Guest'
Syllable count: 3, 3, 7, 3, 3, 4, 5

    Seeing the
    Red petals
    Lying in the misty court,
    I drop my
    Sewing, and
    Like the weeping
    Willow, long for love.

二十四. 迎仙客　　李致遠

暮春
吹落紅
棟花風
深院垂楊輕霧中
小窗閒
停繡工
簾幙重重
不鎖相思夢

25

Author: Liu Chih
Title: 'Fond Farewell'
Tune: 'A Goose Falls' with 'Song
　　　　of Victory'
Syllable count: 5, 5, 5, 5, 5, 5, 5, 5, 2, 5, 2, 5

　　As warm winds excite
　　Swallows and Orioles,
　　Soft sunbeams bathe peach
　　Bloom and apricot.
　　The river Yangtze
　　Marks a silvery
　　Line. Hills far distant
　　Repose after rain.
　　With wine
　　And willow branch, I
　　Honour
　　Your parting from Wei.

二十五. 雁兒落帶得勝令　　　劉　致

和風閙燕鶯　　夢裡思梁苑
麗日明桃杏　　花時別渭城
長江一線平　　長亭
暮雨千山靜　　咫尺人孤另
載酒送君行　　愁聽
折柳繫離情　　陽關第四聲

Author: Ma Chiu-kao
Title: 'Thinking of the Past at Ling-chiao's Tower'
Tune: 'Wild Goose in Autumn Outside the
　　　　Great Wall'
Syllable count: 7, 7, 7, 7, 5, 5, 7

　　　Near these yellow hills once lived
　　　A gay folk. At Wu-river
　　　Ford, below, our beaten troops
　　　Crossed. Clouds obscure the evening
　　　Sun. Yet Li Po's tomb
　　　In its green springtime
　　　Remains token to our fame.

二十六.塞鴻秋　　　　馬九皋
　　　凌歊臺懷古
凌歊臺畔黃山鋪
是三千歌舞士家處
望夫山下烏江渡
是八千子弟思鄉去
江東日暮雲
渭北春天樹
青山太白墳如故

Author: Ma Chiu-kao
Title: 'Collating Ancient Verse'
Tune: 'Water Fairy'
Syllable count: 7, 7, 7, 8, 7, 5, 5, 5

Idle for years, beside rivers
And lakes, I have drunk from Lord
Huang's cup. Sad thoughts cannot
Penetrate Liu Ling's tomb. For in
Drunken lands fools and savants
Rank same. Romantics
View our mountains, or
Pledge themselves to drink.

二十七．水仙子　　馬九皋
　　　集古
幾年無事傍江湖
醉倒黃公舊酒壚
人間縱有傷心處
也不到劉伶墳上土
醉鄉中不辨賢愚
對風流人物
看江山畫圖
不醉倒何如

Author: Jen Yü
Title: 'Harmonizing with a Friend's Rhyme'
Tune: 'Red Embroidered Shoes'
Syllable count: 6, 6, 7, 5, 5, 6

   Grass huts fall before strong
   Winds. The moon soars vainly
   Over cinnamons. Gladly
   I plan to retire.
   Friends in the tiger's
   Tent should not miss me much.

二十八. 紅繡鞋　　　任昱

和友人韻

茅屋秋風吹破
桂叢夜月空過
淮南招隱故情多
無心登虎帳
有夢到漁簑
不歸來等甚麼

29

Author: Jen Yü
Title: 'Lying Low'
Tune: 'Heavily Drunk in the East Wind'
Syllable count: 6, 6, 3, 3, 7, 7, 7

Beautiful mountains and
Rivers abide the years.
Eastern troops
Arrive, as
Western troops get drunk. Fishers,
Woodsmen, talk. I shall not send
My portrait to the palace.

二十九. 沉醉東風　　任昱

有待江山信美
無情歲月相催
東里來
西鄰醉
聽漁樵講些興廢
依舊中原一布衣
更休想麒麟畫裡

Author: Ch'a Te-ch'ing
Title: 'Heroes of the Past'
Tune: 'Cinnamon Breaking Song'
Syllable count: 7, 4, 4, 4, 4, 4, 7, 7, 4, 4, 4, 4

Who were our heroes? Fishers,
Farmers, hiding
At Nan-yang. With
One stroke they won!
Their strategy
Of eight fronts worked!
Fei-hsiung and Wo-Lung felled kings.
Yet regrets were without end.
The Shu road, clothed
In cold clouds, and
The Wei river,
Bode Autumn winds.

三十. 折桂令　　　查德卿
　　　　懷　古
問從來誰是英雄　八陣圖名成臥龍
一個農夫　　　　六韜書功在飛熊
一個漁翁　　　　霸業成空
晦跡南陽　　　　遺恨無窮
棲身東海　　　　蜀道寒雲
一舉成功　　　　渭水秋風

Author: Lu Chih
Title: 'Landscape'
Tune: 'Heavily Drunk in the East Wind'
Syllable count: 7, 7, 5, 5, 7, 7, 7

Withered pines project from cliffs
Against the evening clouds which
Race now the lone duck.
Endless mountains, broad
Rivers, sadly share Autumn.
This scene reminds me of my
Most cherished paintings at home.

三十一. 沉醉東風　　盧摯

挂絕壁枯松倒倚
落殘霞孤鶩齊飛
四圍不盡山
一望無窮水
散西風滿天秋意
夜靜雲帆月影低
載我在瀟湘畫裡

Author: Ma Chih-yüan
Title: 'Homecoming'
Tune: 'Four Pieces of Jade'
Syllable count: 3, 3, 7, 7, 6, 6, 3

Bearing fresh
Fish, new wine,
I view cloudy mountains. Brisk
Winds, pale moons, repay a poet's
Debts. Basically carefree,
Without courtier's talents,
I return.

三十二. 四塊玉　　馬致遠

沽買　
旋新　
酒魚滿眼雲山畫圖開
　　清風明月還詩債
　　本是個懶散人
　　又無甚經濟才
　　歸去來

33

Author: Ma Chih-yüan
Title: 'Query'
Tune: 'Plucking Cannot Harm It'
Syllable count: 3, 3, 7, 7, 7, 4

　　Wearing plain
　　Clothes, I ask:
　　What good are palaces? Tombs
　　Of our kings grow Catalpas.
　　Tungs garnish official ruins.
　　Yet nightmares reign!

三十三. 撥不斷　馬致遠

　　布衣中
　　問英雄
　　王圖霸業成何用
　　禾黍高低六代宮
　　楸梧遠近千官塚
　　一場惡夢

34

Author: Chang K'e-chiu
Title: 'Sadness in Spring'
Tune: 'Four Pieces of Jade'
Syllable count: 3, 3, 7, 7, 3, 3, 3

    Awake from
    Morning dreams,
    Make-up still caked, I miss my
    Young man. Long absent, he brings
    To mind, blue
    Rivers, ripe
    Fruit, green grass.

三十四. 四塊玉　　張可久

春愁

曉夢雲
殘粧粉
一點芳心怨王孫
十年不寄平安信
綠水濱
碧草春
紅杏村

35

Author: Chang K'e-chiu
Title: 'Thoughts in Autumn'
Tune: 'Water Fairy'
Syllable count: 7, 7, 7, 5, 6, 3, 3, 4

Geese lace cold white clouds. Jade
Faced girl, inspecting myself,
Gusty Autumn winds suggest you!
Singing sadly, I
Drink wine. So trim life's wick
To its end!
Drinking to
You this sad evening.

三十五. 水仙子　　　張可久
　　　　秋　思
天邊白雁寫寒雲
鏡裡青鸞瘦玉人
秋風昨夜愁成陣
思君不見君
緩歌獨自開樽
燈挑盡
酒半醺
如此黃昏

Author: Hsü Tsai-ssu
Title: 'Nonconformist'
Tune: 'Red Silk Robe'
Syllable count: 6, 6, 6, 5, 5, 6, 6, 6

Leisure loving old man,
He fishes the snowy
River. In full moon,
Thoughtless of Emperors,
He sails. Beloved of
One, he brought his baited
Hook toward the palace: turned,
And went back to Fu-ch'un.

三十六. 紅錦袍　　徐再思

那老子愛清閒主意別
釣桐江江上雪
泛桐江江上月
君王想念者
宣到鳳凰闕
想着七里漁灘
將着一鈎香餌
望着富春山歸去也

Author: Chang K'e-chiu
Title: 'Spring Night'
Tune: 'Red Embroidered Shoes'
Syllable count: 6, 6, 7, 5, 5, 5

Wine-sick poet, midst blossoms
And birds, I compose songs
To Moons after rains—plucking
Ice from the creek to
Chill my drink before
I play my zither.

三十七. 紅繡鞋　　張可久

春　夜

燕子來時病酒
牡丹開處詩情
庭院黃昏雨初晴
鏡心閒掛月
箏手碎彈冰
尊前春夜永

Author: Chang K'e-chiu
Title: 'Sad Thoughts in Spring'
Tune: 'Audience with the King'
Syllable count: 5, 5, 5, 7, 5, 4, 4, 6, 2, 2, 6

Flower-shaped mirrors crack.
Lutes lack strings. Friends help'd,
Are now fierce. Swallows
Returning each year cannot
Counsel the lone goose,
As she sees that
The tomb is swept
Clean. How sadly she sails
Toward it,
Hiding
Her pale face in passing.

三十八. 朝天子　　張可久
　　　春　思

菱花破雨邊
瑤琴斷四弦
恩又番成怨
黃雲孤雁褪花鈿
羞掩雙鸞扇

歸燕年年
離恨綿綿
又西湖拜掃天
寺前
上船
試照我傷春面

Author: Chang K'e-chiu
Title: 'Autumn Dream'
Tune: 'The Pure River Flows'
Syllable count: 7, 5, 5, 5, 7

 West winds bring letters asking
 My return. Wild geese
 Honk above Autumn
 Leaves in this drunk-dream,
 Midst warm, rain-washed banana palms.

三十九. 清江引   張可久
   秋　懷

西風信來家萬里
問我歸期未
雁啼紅葉天
人醉黃花地
芭蕉雨聲秋夢裡

40

Author: Chang K'e-chiu
Title: 'Thinking in Autumn'
Tune: 'Happiness to the Wide World'
Syllable count: 3, 3, 4, 4, 5, 5, 7, 7, 4, 4, 4

    Employed by
    Fate as West
    Winds howl, at inns
    I dismount. By
    Lamp-light I reflect:
    Under blue skies the
    Shu road is hard for seekers
    Of fame. My white hairs suggest
    Friends, now dead, who
    Fished and gardened,
    And would have laughed.

四十．普天樂　　　　張可久
　　　　秋　懷

爲誰忙　　　　兩字功名頻看鏡
莫非命　　　　不饒人白髮星星
西風驛馬　　　釣魚子陵
落月書燈　　　思蓴季鷹
青天蜀道難　　笑我飄零
紅葉吳江冷

Author: Ch'iao Chi
Title: 'On Visiting Prince Yueh-fu's Estate'
Tune: 'Water Fairy'
Syllable count: 7, 7, 7, 6, 7, 6, 6, 4

    With flute songs dreams now sink
    In thorny sands. The fragrance
    Of silken bed clothes is now
    Replaced by fern-smell. Wild clouds,
    Old trees, setting suns, combine
    With swallows to suggest
    That broken pavilions
    Tell signs of loss.

四十一. 水仙子　　喬吉
　　　遊越福王府

笙歌夢斷蒺藜沙
羅綺香餘野菜花
亂雲老樹夕陽下
燕休尋王謝家
恨興亡怒煞些鳴蛙
鋪錦池理荒甃
流杯亭堆破瓦
何處也繁華

Author: Ch'iao Chi
Title: 'The Ruins of Yüeh'
Tune: 'Cinnamon Breaking Song'
Syllable count: 6, 4, 4, 4, 4, 4, 4, 6, 4, 6, 4, 4, 4

> Midst ochre dust, by rice
> Fields ringed, where hares
> Dodge foxes—'neath
> Blue clouds, these stones
> Mark the fates of
> Eastern kings. Gone
> Are brave Yu-chün,
> The king's sword, and the fair
> Hsi-shih. Hoarsely,
> Cuckoos break the
> Silence. There's no
> More Spring in this,
> My native land!

四十二．折桂令　　　　　喬吉
　　丙子游越懷古

蓬萊老樹蒼雲　　東晉亡也
禾黍高低　　　　再難尋個右軍
狐兔紛紜　　　　西施去也
半折殘碑　　　　絕不見甚佳人
空餘故址　　　　海氣長昏
總是黃塵　　　　啼鴂聲乾
　　　　　　　　天地無春

Author: Wang Yun
Title: 'Evening Scene'
Tune: 'Little Red Peach'
Syllable count: 7, 5, 7, 3, 7, 4, 4, 5

Words of lotus pickers mix
With cool Autumn's smoke.
Wakes from orchid boats subside.
Should such scenes
Of this beautiful land last
An old foreign
Man the rest of
His declining years?

四十三. 小桃紅　　王惲

採蓮人語隔秋煙
波靜如橫練
入手風光莫流轉
共流連
畫船一笑春風面
江山信美
終非吾土
何日是歸年

Author: Kuan Yun-shih
Title: 'Renascence'
Tune: 'Joy in Front of the Palace'
Syllable count: 3, 7, 7, 4, 5, 3, 5, 4, 4

Gentle winds
Waft voices of flower-sellers
Into my garden after
Rain. Walking the
Flowered path I savour
The dampness.
Pausing beneath the
Blossoms, I think
A new Spring-thought.

四十四. 殿前歡　　貫雲石

隔簾聽
幾番風送賣花聲
夜來微雨天階靜
小院閒庭
輕寒翠袖生
穿芳徑
十二欄杆凭
杏花疎影
楊柳新情

45

Author: Anonymous
Title: 'Sad Courtesan'
Tune: 'Pure River Flows'
Syllable count: 7, 5, 5, 5, 7

   Sad winds sough through empty courts.
   Peach blossoms fall. My
   Lover is lost—or
   Has fled—beyond the
   Spring-green hills which I now view.

四十五. 清江引　　　無名

樓頭柳絲風力軟
寂寞閒庭院
獨自倚欄杆
落盡桃花片
青山不知郎近遠

Author: Sun Chou-ch'ing
Title: 'Courtesan's Song'
Tunes: 'Scolding the Jade Boy' with 'Gratitude for the
 Emperor's Grace' and 'Tea Plucking Song'
Syllable count: 7, 3, 3, 7, 3, 3, 3; 4, 4, 3, 3, 3, 4, 4, 3, 3, 3;
 3, 3, 7, 7, 7

Showered swings at sunset, this
Spring evening,
Suggest tears.
Green clouds obscure Hang Hai's road.
The Phoenix
Flees. Swallows
Mingle with

Orioles. Live
Jealousies lurk
By towers.
Grass smoke spreads.
Snow flowers
Dance, cavorting
With willowed winds.
Like beloved
Fair flowers,
I grow thin.

Pale, in gold
Combs, in green
Feathers, and scented pearls, in
Silk brocades, I read his sealed
Note, and pause beside the rail.

四十六．罵玉郎帶感皇恩採茶歌　　孫周卿

院宇春將暮

淚珠隔斷陽臺路

朱孤疏妬

階亭鋪舞扶我花梳羽

除陽癱腋

珠襦書封歸無語

淚到期空慢

曹自敷

無數踏

千滴淚浴雲鳳燕鸞步立煙雪風驚愛盒翠香雞箋時指欄

秋紅綠朝去來流懶倦草梨柳花我玉金寶繡錦富屈倚

Author: Chung Ssu-ch'eng
Title: 'Sad Spring Song'
Tunes: 'Scolding the Jade Boy' with 'Gratitude for the
Emperor's Grace' and 'Tea Plucking Song'
Syllable count: 7, 3, 3, 7, 3, 3, 3: 4, 4, 3, 3, 3, 4, 4, 3, 3, 3:
3, 3, 7, 7, 7

Plum blossoms tell me Spring is
Here. East Winds
Now melt snows.
Festivals approach with warm
Weather!
Fragrant drunks
Now wander.

In small towns, Spring
Urges willows
To bear fruit.
Cuckoos sing
Because it's
Spring. Fields can now
Blossom, two parts
Water, one
Part dust. In
Quiet, when

Flowers have
Fallen, I
Feel sad. Midst fragrant grass, I
Breathe the aromas, and still
Enjoying them, I fear death!

四十七.罵玉郎帶感皇恩採茶歌　　鍾嗣成

春

梅花漏泄陽和信
才殘臘
又新春
東風北岸冰消盡
元夜過
社日臨
中和近
天氣氤氳
花柳精神
駕香輪
馳玉勒
醉遊人
清明過了
飛絮紛紛
隔孤村
聞杜宇
怨東君
嘆芳辰
已三分
二分流水一分塵
寂寞落花傷暮景
淒淒芳草怕黃昏

48

Song Chain I

Author: Kuan Han-ch'ing
Mode: 'Hsien-lü'
Title: 'Tears from the Boudoir'

48A—*Tune:* 'Jade Green Skirt at Her Waist'
Syllable count: 7, 5, 7, 3, 7

>Mountain rains swell rivers. From
>The tower I view the
>Flood. Every Autumn our
>World becomes
>Evening, as islands drown.

48B—*Tune:* 'The Liu-yao Song'
Syllable count: 4, 3, 4, 4, 4, 4, 6, 2, 8

>Chill West winds cause
>Tungs to drop
>Their leaves. Summer
>Leaves its fragrant
>Scent. My ink screen
>Represents this
>Season. But the crickets
>Must be
>Live, in the willows, to add sound.

四十八. 套數 (一)　　　關漢卿
　　　　　閨　怨

(翠裙腰) 曉來雨過山橫秀
　　　　野水漲汀洲
　　　　闌干倚遍空回首
　　　　下危樓
　　　　一天風物暮傷秋
(六么遍) 乍涼時候
　　　　西風透
　　　　碧梧脫葉
　　　　餘暑才收
　　　　香生鳳口
　　　　簾垂玉鉤
　　　　小院深閒清晝
　　　　清幽
　　　　聽聲聲蟬噪柳梢頭

48C—*Tune:* 'Parasitic Grass'
   Syllable count: 3, 3, 7, 7, 7, 5, 5

   Should wives weep
   For absent
   Husbands, when jade mirrors bear
   Dust, when sewing no longer
   Suffices, when bracelets come
   Loose, when foreheads are
   Wrinkled? I say yes!

48D—*Tune:* 'Capitol-Bound Horse'
   Syllable count: 3, 5, 7, 4, 6

   With whom does
   He hold hands and drink,
   And sing behind green screens? I
   Have forgotten
   My fierce words, and his name!

48E—*Tune:* last stanza of 'The Rear Garden
         Flower'
   Syllable count: 5, 5, 5, 5, 3, 4, 7

   I hide my face with
   My sleeve and pour the
   Sad wine. I should have
   My walls painted, or
   Forget the
   Silken words he
   Spoke without thought.

（寄生草）為甚憂
為甚愁
為蕭郎一去經今久
玉臺寶鑑生塵垢
綠窗冷落閒針繡
豈知人玉腕釧兒鬆
豈知人兩葉眉兒皺
（上京馬）他何處
共誰人攜手
小閣銀屏瑞歌酒
早忘了呪
不記得低低籌
（後庭花煞）掩袖暗含羞
開樽越釀愁畫
悶把錦字修
最風流
真真恩愛
等閒分付等閒休

49

Song Chain II

Author: Po P'u
Mode: 'Hsien-lü'
Title: 'Sad Wives and Courtesans'

49A—*Tune:* 'Paint the Red Lips'
Syllable count: 4, 4, 3, 4, 5, 4, 5, 3, 4, 5

> I remove my
> Gold hairpins. My
> Husband rides
> To the city.
> Brisk Autumn suggests
> I stop sewing
> And view from our tower,
> Mountain clouds
> More beautiful
> Than those in fine prints.

49B—*Tune:* 'Mud River Dragon'
Syllable count: 4, 7, 4, 4, 7, 7, 3, 4, 4

> My heart breaks twice.
> At the heavenly sunset
> Near the river's
> Edge. Now geese sleep
> Midst dry lotus. Crows nod on
> Their branches. Bamboos pattern
> My screens. Midst
> Mortar sounds, I
> Play my sad lute.

四十九. 套數 (二)　　　白樸

(仙呂)

【點絳唇】金鳳釵分，玉京人去，瀟灑閒暇，晚來收拾樓簾罷，針線倚危珠簾掛。獨二蕭晴雲山，十目人腸處，風雨極斷，照殘宿樓，乍如畫。

【混江龍】斷天枯遠，敗修黃愁怨。荷樹葉竹昏生入，殘宿樓紛珊近砧，鶯鴇紛紛擁掃杵琶，水邊霞，砌石窗紗。

49C—*Tune:* 'Window-Penetrating Moon'
Syllable count: 7, 6, 7, 3, 3, 8

    I think of that crazy old
    Man—riding his green horse,
    While others complain of him.
    His brothel
    Wine, my sad
    Tea, commemorate our lost youth.

49D—*Tune:* 'Parasitic Grass'
Syllable count: 3, 3, 8, 7, 8, 8, 8

    Waiting too
    Long, I turn
    From the tower. Descending the steps
    Barefoot, I feel cold. With wet
    Kerchief, I daub my white powder.
    Jade hairpins, fashionably-bound
    Feet, are the lot of sad young wives.

49E—*Tune:* 'The Yüan-ho Song'
Syllable count: 5, 5, 7, 5, 8, 6

    You have not written.
    The tortoise is mute!
    My eyebrows show sadness. Pale,
    Despite festivals,
    I wonder why you have not yet
    Returned as you promised.

（賞窗月）憶疎狂阻隔天涯
怎知人埋怨他
吟鞭醉裊青驄馬
羹飲秦樓酒
謝家茶
不思量執手臨歧話

（寄生草）凭欄久
歸繡閣
下危樓強把金蓮撒
深沉院宇冷透凌波襪
立蒼苔冷透畫短瓊簪
數歸期空頻濕香羅帕
搵啼痕頻濕香羅帕

（元和令）一從絕雁書
幾度結遍卦
翠眉長是鎖離愁
玉容憔悴煞
目無宵等待過重陽
甚猶然不到家

49F—*Tune:* 'Charm While Mounting the Horse'
Syllable count: 3, 3, 5, 7, 4, 8

    Happiness
    Gets entwined
    In balls of hemp. Walks
    Under the East wall help but
    Little, since the
    Yellow flowers are also sad.

（上馬嬌煞）歡會少　煩惱多
心緒亂如麻
偶然行至東籬下
自嗟自呀
冷清清和月對黃花

50

Song Chain III

Author: Ma Chih-yüan
Mode: 'Shuang-tiao'
Title: 'Autumn'

50A—*Tune:* 'Running a Boat at Night'
Syllable count: 7, 7, 4, 4, 7

    Centuries pass with dreams of
    Butterflies. Pasts have been sad.
    Today's Springs point
    Toward future frosts.
    But wine still can warm us some.

50B—*Tune:* 'Evergreen-tree Song'
Syllable count: 5, 5, 3, 5, 3, 3, 4

    Fishers and woodsmen
    Can't tell dragons from
    Snakes these days.
    At ruins of Chin,
    At Han tombs,
    Where sheep graze,
    Grass covers all!

50C—*Tune:* 'Celebrating the Yüan Ho'
Syllable count: 7, 4, 7, 4

    Though tripods are strong, break one
    Leg, and each falls.
    Wei or Chin, their vassals have
    Grown thin and wise.

五十　套數 (三)　　　馬致遠
　　　　　　秋　思
(雙調)
(夜行船) 百歲光陰一夢蝶
　　　　重回首往事堪嗟
　　　　今日春來
　　　　明朝花謝
　　　　急罰盞夜闌燈滅
(喬木查) 想秦宮漢闕
　　　　都做了衰草牛羊野
　　　　不恁麼漁樵沒話說
　　　　縱荒墳
　　　　橫斷碑
　　　　不辨龍蛇
(慶元和) 投至狐蹤與兔穴
　　　　多少豪傑
　　　　鼎足雖堅半腰折
　　　　魏耶晉耶

50—D *Tune:* 'Plum-Falling Wind'
Syllable count: 3, 3, 7, 3, 6, 7

    Heaven-sent
    Wealth should be
    Savoured. Yet iron spooned children
    Must recoup
    Those good times, well-spent, that
    Their fathers remember sadly.

50E—*Tune:* 'Wind Entering the Pines'
Syllable count: 7, 5, 7, 7, 6, 7

    Before my eyes the sun slants
    West. In my glass I
    See new white hairs. Retiring
    One must disrobe. Owls appear
    Clumsy in daylight. But
    At night they remain supreme.

50F—*Tune:* 'Plucking can't Harm It'
Syllable count: 3, 3, 7, 7, 7, 4

    Discarding
    Honours I
    Remain inside my house. I
    Look out through the cracks in my
    Walls to view bamboo fences,
    And peasant huts.

(落梅風) 天教你富
莫太奢
沒多時好天良夜
富家兒
更做道你心似鐵
爭辜負了錦堂風月
(風入松) 眼前紅日又西斜
疾似下坡車
不爭鏡裡添白雪
上床與鞋履相別
休笑巢鳩計拙
葫蘆提一向裝呆
(撥不斷) 利名竭
是非絕
紅塵不向門前惹
綠樹偏宜屋角遮
青山正補牆頭缺
更那堪竹籬茅舍

50G—*Tune:* 'Feast at the Departing Pavilion' with
last stanza of 'The Hsieh-chih Tune'
Syllable count: 8, 8, 4, 6, 6, 6, 5, 5, 5, 5, 5, 5,
6, 6, 7, 6, 6

Crickets cease chirping—I sleep. At
Dawn the treadmill begins. Ants war!
Bees build hives! Flies
Lap blood! In P'ei's hall, in
T'ao's fine club, I think of
My yellow flowers, my
Fine crabs, my warm wine.
If, at each ninth year,
One could drink Autumn
Leaves, one would be well
Drunk. Then when Pei'-hai
Came to visit—one
Could tell him that Tung-li
Had become indisposed
In good cause! For Autumn's the
Time of festivals that
Calendars cannot count.

（離亭宴帶歇指煞）

蛩吟罷一覺才寧貼
雞鳴時萬事無休歇
何年是徹
看密匝匝蟻排兵
亂紛紛蜂釀蜜
急攘攘蠅爭血
裴公綠野堂
陶令白蓮社
愛秋來時那些
和露摘黃花
帶霜分紫蟹
煮酒燒紅葉
想人生有限杯
渾幾個重陽節
人間我頑童記者
便北海探吾來
道東籬醉了也

APPENDICES TO THE 50 POEMS

The superior numbers refer to the tones in modern Chinese. See p. 140.

POEM 1: *Transliterated*
Author: Kuan Han-ch'ing
Title: 'Pieh²ch'ing²'
Tune: 'Ssu⁴-k'uai⁴-yü⁴'

1. tzu⁴ sung⁴ pieh²	3r
2. hsin¹ nan² she³	3r
3. i¹-tien³ hsiang¹-ssu¹ chi³-shih² chüeh²	7r
4. p'ing²-lan² hsiu⁴ fo² yang²-hua¹ hsüeh³	7r
5. hsi¹ yu⁴ hsieh²	3r
6. shan¹ yu⁴ che²	3r
7. jen² ch'ü⁴ yeh³	3r

1: *Word by word*

1. Since/sending/farewell,
2. (My) heart/is difficult/to bear (cast off),
3. A bit/mutual/love (longing)/when (what time)/ends (cut off)?
4. Leaning (against)/the banister/sleeves/brush off/willow/flower/snow.
5. The stream/again(both)/winding
6. The hill/also/is blocking (the view).
7. The man (person)/has gone!

1: *First draft*

Since farewell,
My heart cannot bear
This bit of mutual longing, when will it come to an end?
Leaning on the banister, my sleeves brush off the snow-white catkins.
The river is winding,
The hill is blocking my view,
The person has gone!

POEM 2: *Transliterated*
Author: Po P'u
Title: 'Chüan⁴ yin³'
Tune: 'Chi⁴-sheng²-ts'ao³'

1. ch'ang² tsui⁴ hou⁴, fang² ho² ai⁴	6
2. pu⁴ hsing³ shih,² yu³ shen⁴ ssu¹	6r
3. tsao¹ yen¹ liang³-ke⁴ kung¹-ming² tzu⁴	7r
4. p'u³ yen¹ ch'ien¹ ku³ hsing¹ wang² shih⁴	7r
5. ch'ü¹ mai¹ wang⁴ chang⁴ hung²-ni² chih⁴	7r
6. pu⁴ ta² shih² chieh¹ hsiao⁴ Ch'ü¹ Yüan² fei¹	8
7. tan⁴ chih¹-yin¹ chin⁴ shuo¹ T'ao² Ch'ien¹ shih⁴	8r

2: *Word by word*

1. Long/drunkness/afterwards/bother/how/hinder?
2. Not/sober/time, is (has) there/what/thinking?
3. (The) dregs/spoil/two/merit-fame/characters (words).
4. (The) unstrained spirits/drowned/thousand-year/rise-fall/events.
5. (The) wine/buried/ten-thousand-feet/rainbow(high)/ambitions.
6. Not/met with/time/all/laugh at/Ch'ü Yüan/wrong.
7. But/knowing/tune/all/(would)say/T'ao Ch'ien/right.

2: *First draft*

After one's drunk, what does it matter?
When one cannot get sober, what thought would he have?
The dregs have already spoiled the two words—merit and fame.
The unstrained spirits have drowned the ups and downs of a thousand years.
And wine has buried my rainbow-high ambitions.
When unsuccessful, one would laugh at Ch'ü Yüan for his wrongs.
To friends, T'ao Ch'ien was quite right.

2: *Notes*

T'ao Ch'ien (AD 365–427) was perhaps the greatest poet in the history of Chinese literature. He lived during the Wei dynasty, and was known as a virtuous man. He served his ruler briefly as a local magistrate, but resigned after only eighty days, refusing to 'break his waist' (to bow) to his superiors for the sake of five bushels of rice per month. He lived subsequently in poverty as a hermit, devoting himself to the writing of poetry.

Ch'ü Yüan is perhaps the first known Chinese poet. He lived during the period of the Warring States (c. 400 BC), and was a faithful and loyal advisor to the king of the State of Ch'u. Slandered by enemies in the Ch'u Court, he was subsequently banished. Hurt and frustrated, he drowned himself in the Milo River after having composed the famous poem titled *Li-sao* (*Encountering Sorrow*).

POEM 3: *Transliterated*

Author: Po P'u
Tune: 'Ch'ing$_4$-tung$_1$-yüan$_2$'

1. wang$_4$-yu$_1$ ts'ao$_3$ 3
2. han$_2$-hsiao$_4$ hua$_1$ 3r
3. ch'üan$_4$ chün$_1$ wen$_2$ tsao$_3$ kuan$_1$ i$_2$ kua$_4$ 7r
4. na$_3$-li$_3$ yeh$_3$ neng$_2$ yen$_2$ Lu$_4$ Chia$_3$ 7r
5. na$_3$-li$_3$ yeh$_3$ liang$_2$ mou$_2$ Tzu$_3$-ya$_2$ 7r
6. na$_3$-li$_3$ yeh$_3$ hao$_2$-ch'i$_4$ Chang$_1$ Hua$_2$ 7r
7. ch'ien$_1$-ku$_3$ shih$_4$-fei$_1$ hsin$_1$ 5
8. i$_1$-hsi$_2$ yü$_2$ ch'iao$_2$ hua$_4$ 5r

3: *Word by word*

1. Forget/worries/grass,
2. Contain/smile/flower,
3. Advise/you/early/cap(hat)/fit/(to be) hanged.
4. Where (is)/can talk(eloquent)/Lu Chia?
5. Where (is)/good counselling/Tsu-ya?
6. Where (is)/(the) heroic/Chang Hua?
7. Thousand ages/right/wrong/mind(intention),
8. One/evening's/fisherman/woodsman's/chat.

3: *First draft*

Like the carefree grass,
And the ever-smiling flower,
I advise you to hang up your (official)cap early.
Where was the eloquent Lu Chia?
Where was that good counsellor, Tzu-ya?
Where was that heroic Chang Hua?
The intentions, right or wrong, of the thousand ages
Are but an evening's chat of fisherman and woodsmen.

3: *Notes*

Lu Chia lived in Han during the reign of Emperor Kao-ti (c. 206 BC). He aided the Emperor in consolidating power. Lu Chia was known as an eloquent and skilful debater. His biography is available in the *Shih-chi (Historical Record)*.

Tzu-ya refers to Chiang Tzu-ya, the prime minister to King Wen of Chou (c. 1122 BC).

Chang Hua lived at Chin in the time of Emperor Wu-ti (c. 140–86 BC). He was given the office of *chung-shu-ling* (Chief Secretary to the Emperor). He was known for his literary talents and for his effective efforts in recruiting others to governmental service. His biography is available in the *Chin shu (History of Chin)*.

POEM 4: *Transliterated*

Author: Po P'u
Title: 'Yü^2-fu^4 tz'u^2'
Tune: 'Ch'en^2-tsui^4-tung^1-feng^1'

1. huang^2-lu^2 an^4 pai^2-p'in^2 tu^4-k'ou^3	7r
2. lü^4-yang^2 ti^1 hung^2-liao^4 t'an^1-t'ou^2	7r
3. sui^1 wu^2 wen^3-ching^4 chiao^1	5
4. ch'üeh^4 yu^3 wang^4-chi^1 yu^3	5r
5. tien^3 ch'iu^1-chiang^1 pai^2-lu^4 sha^1-ou^1	7r
6. ao^4-sha^1 jen^2-chien^1 wan^4-hu^4-hou^2	7r
7. pu^1 shih^4-tzu^4 yen^1-p'o^1 tiao^4-sou^3	7r

4: *Word by word*
1. Yellow/reeds/shore,/white/ duckweeds/ferry,
2. Green/willows/dyke/ red/smartweed/beachhead.
3. Though/have no/neck-cutting/friends,
4. But/have/time-forgetting/acquaintance.
5. Touching/autumn/river/white/cranes/sandy/gulls.
6. Prouder(than)/human world's/ten-thousand/families/dukes.
7. Not/know/characters/smoky/waves/fishing/old man.

4: *First draft*
By the shore of the yellow reeds and at the white duckweed ferry,
Along the dyke of green willows and the beach of red smartweed,
Though he has no intimate friends who would die for him,
He has acquaintance who would ignore the time—
Those white cranes and sandy gulls dipping on the autumn river.
Prouder than the dukes of the human world supported by ten thousand families
Is the illiterate old fisherman of the smoky waves.

POEM 5: *Transliterated*

Author: Yang Kuo
Title: 'Ts'ai^3 lien^2 ko^1' I
Tune: 'Hsiao^3-t'ao^2-hung^2'

1. ts'ai^3-lien^2 jen^2 ho^2 ts'ai^3-lien^2 ko^1 7r
2. liu^3 wai^4 lan^2-chou^1 kuo^4 5r
3. pu^4-kuan^3 yüan^1-yang^1 meng^4 ching^1-p'o^4 7r
4. yeh^4 ju^2-ho^2 3r
5. yu^3-jen^1 tu^2 shang^4 chiang^1-lou^2 wo^4 7r
6. shang^1-hsin^1 mo^4 ch'ang^4 4
7. Nan^2-ch'ao^2 chiu^4 ch'ü^3 4
8. Ssu^1-ma^3 lei^4 hen^2 to^1 5r

5: *Word by word*
1. pluck/lotus/person/and/pluck/lotus/song,
2. Willows/beyond/orchid/boat/passes.
3. Disregard/mandarin ducks/dream/startled/broken
4. Night/how(was)?
5. Someone/alone/climbed up/river/tower/(and)lying down.
6. Heart-broken/don't/sing
7. Southern/dynasties/old/tunes.
8. Ssu-ma/tears/plenty.

5: *First draft*
The lotus-plucking person and the lotus-plucking song
Pass beyond the willows in an orchid boat.

Heedless about breaking my dream of lovers.
How was the night?
Someone went up alone to the river tower and lay there.
If heart-broken, don't sing
The tunes of the southern dynasties.
The tears of Ssu-ma were so much!

POEM 6: *Transliterated*

Author: Yang Kuo
Title: 'Ts'ai$_3$ lien^2 ko^{1}' II
Tune: 'Hsiao$_3$-t'ao^2-hung^{2}'

1. ts'ai$_3$-lien^2 hu^2 shang$_4$ cho^1 ch'uan^2 hui^2 7r
2. feng^1 yüeh^1 Hsiang^1-ch'ün^2 ts'ui$_4$ 5r
3. i^1-chü$_3$ p'i^2-pa^1 shu$_4$-hang^2 lei$_4$ 7r
4. wang$_4$ chün^1 kui^1 3r
5. fu^2-jung^2 k'ai^1 chin$_4$ wu^2 hsiao^1-hsi$_4$ 7r
6. wan$_3$-liang^2 to^1-shao$_3$ 4
7. hung^2-yüan^1 pai$_2$-lu$_4$ 4
8. ho^2-ch'u$_4$ pu$_4$ shuang^1 fei^1 5r

6: *Word by word*

1. Pluck/lotus/lake/on/boats/passed,
2. (The) wind/gentle/(the) Hsiang/skirt/green.
3. One/tune(of)/p'ipa/several/lines/tears,
4. Expecting(hoping)/you/return.
5. Mimosa (flowers)/bloomed/end/without/news
6. Evening/cold/how much.
7. Red/Mandarin ducks/white/cranes
8. Where/not/(in) pairs/fly?

6: *First draft*

On the lotus plucking lake the boats have returned.
The wind is gentle, and the silk skirt is green.
After a tune of p'ipa, many tear stains appear.
I am hoping for your return.
The mimosas have withered, but no news came.
How cold the evening is.
Those red mandarin ducks and white cranes
Where don't they fly in pairs?

POEM 7: *Transliterated*

Author: Hu Chih-yü
Title: 'Ssu$_4$ chi$_4$'
Tune: 'I^1-pan$_4$-erh^{2}'

1. ho²-p'an² chien³ ts'ui⁴ chü²-hua¹ huang²   7r
2. feng¹ yeh⁴ p'iao¹ hung² wu² kan⁴ ts'ang¹   7r
3. yüan¹-pei⁴ pu¹ chin⁴ tso²-yeh⁴ liang²   7r
4. jang³ ch'iu¹-kuang¹   3r
5. i¹-pan⁴-erh² hsi¹-feng¹ i¹-pan⁴-erh² shuang¹   8r

7: *Word by word*
1. Lotus/plate/reduced/greenness/chrysanthemums/yellow,
2. Maple/leaves/float/red/wu-t'ung/trunks/green.
3. Mandarin-duck/quilt/cannot/bear/last night/coldness.
4. Brewing/autumn/scene,
5. One half/west wind/one half/frost.

7: *First draft*
The green has faded from the plate-shaped lotus leaves, and chrysanthemums are yellow.
The maple leaves flicker red, and the wu-t'ung tree trunks are green.
The Mandarin-duck patterned quilt could not keep out the cold of last night.
Indeed the autumn is brewing
Half because of the west wind, half because of the frost.

POEM 8: *Transliterated*

Author: Hu Chih-yü
Title: 'Ssu⁴ chi⁴'
Tune: 'I¹-pan⁴-erh²'

1. ch'ing¹ shan¹ tuan³ mao⁴ ch'i¹-hsiang¹ chü¹   7r
2. chiu³ shih² ch'un¹-kuang¹ ju² hua⁴-t'u²   7r
3. ming²-jih⁴ lo⁴ hung² shui² shih⁴ chu³   7r
4. man⁴ ch'ou²-ch'u⁴   3r
5. i¹-pan⁴-erh² yin¹ feng¹ i¹-pan⁴-erh² yü³   8r

8: *Word by word*
1. Light/shirt/short/hat/seven/fragrance/carriage,
2. Nine(out of)/ten/spring scenes/like/pictures.
3. Tomorrow/fall/red/who/will be/the master?
4. Slowly/hesitate
5. One half/due to/rain/one half/wind.

8: *First draft*
With light shirt, low hat and in its many perfumed carriage,
Nine out of ten spring scenes resemble pictures.
When the red petals fall tomorrow, who would be master?
Don't you worry.
Half because of wind, half because of rain.

POEM 9: *Transliterated*

Author: Yao Sui
Title: 'Kan3 huai2'
Tune: 'Tsui4-kao1-ko1'

1. shih2-nien2 Yen1 yüeh4 ko1-sheng1   6r
2. chi3-tien3 Wu2 shuang1 pin4 ying3   6r
3. hsi1-feng1 ch'ui1 ch'i3 lu2-yü2 hsing4 7r
4. I3 tsai4 sang1 yü2 mu4-ching3   6r

9: *Word by word*
1. Ten/years/Yen(northern)/moon/song/sound,
2. Several/dots/Wu(southern)/frost/temple/shadow.
3. West/wind/blow up/perch's/mood,
4. Already/lies at/mulberry/elm/evening/scene.

9: *First draft*

For ten years I enjoyed the northern moon and its songs.
Several frost-coloured patches of hair show near my temples.
The west wind has quickened the sea perch.
But it is already the scene of evening among the mulberry and elm trees.

POEM 10: *Transliterated*

Author: Yao Sui
Tune: 'Hsi3-ch'un1-lai2'

1. pi3 t'ou2 feng1-yüeh4 shih2-shih2 kuo4   7r
2. yen3 ti3 erh2-ts'ao2 chien4-chien4 to1   7r
3. yu3-jen2 wen4 wo3 shih4 ju2-ho2   7r
4. jen2-hai3 k'uo4   3r
5. wu2-jih4 pu4 feng1 p'o1   5r

10: *Word by word*
1. Brush/end/wind/moon/time-time(frequent)/pass.
2. Eyes/below/children/gradually/more.
3. Someone/asks/me/things(affairs)/how?
4. (The) human/sea/wide,
5. No/day/without/wind/waves.

10: *First draft*

The wind and moon are often caught by the tip of my brush.
But below my eyes children have become more and more numerous.

Someone asks me, 'How Are Things?'
'The human-sea is too wide,' I reply,
'And not one day passes without wind storms.'

POEM 11: *Transliterated*

Author: Ma Chih-yüan
Title: 'Ch'iu¹ ssu¹'
Tune: 'T'ien¹-ching⁴-sha¹'

1. k'u¹-t'eng² lao³-shu⁴ hun¹-ya¹   6r
2. hsiao³-ch'iao² liu²-shui³ jen²-chia¹   6r
3. ku³-tao⁴ hsi¹-feng¹ shou⁴-ma³   6r
4. hsi¹-yang² hsi¹ hsia⁴   4r
5. tuan⁴-ch'ang²-jen² tsai⁴ t'ien¹-ya²   6r

11: *Word by word*

1. Withered/vine/old/tree/evening/crow,
2. Small/bridge/running/stream/people's home.
3. Ancient/road/west/wind/lean/horse,
4. Evening/sun/westward/goes down,
5. Heart-broken/man/at/heaven's edge.

11: *First draft*

Withered vines, I see, an old tree, the evening crow,
A small bridge over a running stream by someone's house.
On the ancient road, in the west wind, is a lean horse.
The evening sun sinks westward.
A heart-broken man is at the edge of heaven.

POEM 12: *Transliterated*

Author: Chang Yang-hao
Title: None
Tune: 'P'u³-t'ien¹-lo⁴'

1. Ch'u³ Li²-sao¹   3
2. shui² neng² chieh³   3r
3. chiu⁴-chung¹ chih¹ i⁴   4
4. jih⁴ yüeh⁴ ming²-pai²   4r
5. hen⁴ shang⁴ ts'un²   3
6. jen² ho² tsai⁴   3r
7. k'ung¹ k'uai⁴-huo² liao³   4
8. Hsiang¹-chiang¹ yü² hsia¹ hsieh⁴   5r
9. che⁴ hsien¹-sheng¹ ch'ang⁴-hao³ (shih⁴) hu²-lai²   7
10. (tsen³ ju² hsiang⁴) ch'ing¹-shan¹ ying³ li³   4
11. k'uang² ke¹ t'ung⁴ yin³   4
12. ch'i² lo⁴ wu²-ya²   4r

12: *Word by word*

1. Ch'u's/Li-sao,
2. Who/can/understand?
3. Within/its/meaning
4. Sun/moon/understand.
5. Regret/still/exists.
6. Man/where/at?
7. Vainly/(being) happy
8. Hsiang/River's/fish/shrimp/crab.
9. This/mister/indeed/misbehaves.
10. (How is like)/among/green/hill/shadow/inside,
11. Madly/drink/painfully/sing
12. Its/happiness/without/limit.

12: *First draft*

The Li-sao of Ch'u
Who could explain?
But its hidden meaning
Is understood by the sun and the moon.
The regret still lingers,
But the man has gone.
Merely happy
Were the fish, shrimp and crab in the Hsiang River.
This man indeed misbehaved.
How would it be in the shadows of the green mountain,
Let's sing madly and drink painfully,
Till our pleasure finds no end.

12: *Note*

Li-sao or 'encountering Sorrow' is a famous Chinese poem written by Ch'ü Yüan of Ch'u during the period of the Warring States in late Chou. Slandered and subsequently banished from the court after faithful and loyal service to his king, Ch'ü in despair drowned himself in the Milo River.

POEM 13. *Transliterated*

Author: Chang Yang-hao
Title: None
Tune: 'Ch'ao^2-t'ien^1-tzu^3'

1.	tzu^4 k'e^4	2
2.	t'ui^4 kui^1	2r
3.	yung^4-pu^4-chao^2 feng^1-yun^2 ch'i^4	6r
4.	shu^1-k'uang^2 yü^1-k'uo^4 chuo^1 yu^4 ch'ih^2	7r
5.	chin^1-jih^4 ts'ai^2 hui^2-wei^4	5r
6.	wan^2-shui^3 yu^2-shan^1	4

7. shen¹ wu² chü¹-hsi⁴	4r
8. (che⁴ ti³ shih⁴) san¹-shih² nien² lo⁴-te²	5r
9. ts'ui⁴ wei¹	2r
10. keng⁴ ch'i²	2r
11. chih¹-tao⁴ wo³ hsien²-chü¹ i⁴	6r

13: *Word by word*

1. Since/impeachment
2. Retreat(withdraw)/return
3. Use/no more/wind-cloud/spirit.
4. Lazy/far-fetching/clumsy/stupid
5. Today/then/realize.
6. roam(along)/waters/play/mountains,
7. (The) body/has no/restriction.
8. (This indeed)/thirty years/ended.
9. Jade/delicate
10. More/strange
11. Know/my/retirement/intentions.

13: *First draft*

Hindered,
I return home.
I no longer need those heaven-soaring ambitions.
Being undisciplined, unruly, clumsy and stupid,
I only realize it today.
Playing along rivers and roaming around mountains,
I have no restrictions.
This is indeed what I have ended up with after thirty years.
The green rivers,
The strange-looking mountains,
Welcome my plans for retirement.

POEM 14: *Transliterated*

Author: Anonymous
Title: None
Tune: 'Hung²-hsiu⁴-hsieh²'

1. Ch'u³ Pa⁴-wang² hsiu¹ k'ua¹ yung³-lieh⁴	7r
2. Han⁴ Kao¹-tsu³ mo⁴ shuo¹ hao²-chieh²	7r
3. (i¹-ke⁴) chü³ ting³ pa²-shan¹ (i¹-ke⁴) chan³ pai²-she²	7r
4. Han⁴ ling² ts'an²-yüeh⁴ chao⁴	5
5. Ch'u³ miao⁴ mu⁴ yun² che¹	5r
6. erh⁴ ying¹-hsiung² ho²-ch'ü⁴ yeh³	6r

14: *Word by word*

1. Ch'u/King Pa/don't/boast/ bravery.
2. Han/(Emperor)Kao-tsu/don't/talk/heroism.
3. One/lifted up/tripod/move/mountains/one/killed/white/serpent.

4. Han/tombs/remaining/moon/shines,
5. Ch'u/temples/evening/dew/covers.
6. Two/heroes/where/at?

14: *First draft*

King Pa of Ch'u, don't you vaunt your bravery.
Emperor Kao-tsu of Han, don't you brag about your heroism.
One lifted the tripod and moved the mountain, one killed a white serpent.
The Han tombs reflect the dim moonlight.
The temples of Ch'u are covered by the evening dew.
Where are those two heroes now?

14: *Notes*

King Pa of Western Ch'u at the close of the Ch'in dynasty contended for control of the country with Liu Pang, the Emperor Kao-tsu of Han. Failing in the contest Pa drowned himself in the Wu River. 'Chu's shrine' in this poem refers back to King Pa.

The Emperor Kao-tsu of Han, also known as Liu Pang, was confronted, according to legend, by a portentous white snake which he killed with his sword. He then went on to raise an army with which he defeated King Pa of Western Ch'u. Liu ultimately succeeded in building the great Han Empire. (As dragons suggest kings, so snakes usually suggest commoners.)

POEM 15: *Transliterated*

Author: Anonymous
Title: 'Hsien² ssu¹'
Tune: 'Chi⁴-sheng¹-ts'ao³'

1. cheng¹ hsien²-ch'i⁴	3r
2. shih³ chien⁴-shih⁴	3r
3. Ch'ih⁴-pi⁴ shan¹ cheng⁴ chung⁴ Chou⁴-lang² chi⁴	8r
4. Wu¹-chiang¹ an⁴ wang⁴ shih³ ch'ung²-t'ung² li⁴	8r
5. Ma³-wei³-p'o¹ k'ung¹ sa³ Ming²-huang² lei⁴	8r
6. ch'ien²-jen² hsün¹-yeh⁴ hou⁴-yen² k'an⁴	7
7. (pu¹ ju²) chin¹-chao¹ tsui⁴ liao³ ming²-chao¹ tsui⁴	7r

15: *Word by word*

1. Fight/idle/anger,
2. Employ/experience.
3. Red-Cliff Mountain/just/fell/Chou-lang's/scheme(plot).
4. Wu River/bank/in vain/used/double eye-pupil/strength.
5. Ma-wei/Slope/in vain/shed/Ming-huang's/tears.
6. Man of past/deeds/later generations/see.
7. (It is not like)Today/get drunk/tomorrow/get drunk.

15: *First draft*

Fighting angrily
And in spite of his experience,
At the Red Cliff Mountain, Chou Lang snared him.
On the bank of Wu River, the one with double eye-pupils made his effort in vain.
On the Ma-wei Slope, Emperor Ming-huang's tears were shed for nothing.
The deeds of men of the past are only for the people of later generations to see.
But for me, I'll get drunk today, and get drunk tomorrow again.

15: *Note*

Chou-lang refers to Chou Yü of Wu State, which was one of the Three Kingdoms (*c.* 200 AD) that fought for control of China near the end of the Han dynasty. The armies of Wu in combination with those of Shu, under Chou Yü as commander of joint forces, defeated with forces of Wei near the site of the Red Cliff.

POEM 16: *Transliterated*

Author: Chang Yang-hao
Title: None
Tune: 'Shih²-erh⁴-yüeh⁴ tai⁴ Yao²-min²-ko¹'

1. ts'ung² t'iao⁴ ch'u¹ kung¹-ming² huo³-k'eng¹   7r
2. lai²-tao⁴ che⁴ hua¹ yüeh⁴ P'eng² Ying²   7r
3. shou³-che¹ che⁴ liang² t'ien² shu⁴ ch'ing³   7r
4. k'an⁴ i¹-hui⁴ yü³-chung⁴ yen¹-keng¹   7r
5. tao⁴-ta⁴-lai² hsin¹-t'ou² pu⁴ ching¹   7r
6. mei³-jih⁴ chia¹ (chih²) shui⁴ tao⁴ t'ien¹-ming²   7r
7. (chien⁴) Hsieh²-ch'uan¹ chi¹ ch'üan³ lo⁴ sheng¹-p'ing² 7r
8. jao³ wu¹ sang¹ ma² ts'ui⁴ yen¹ sheng¹   7r
9. chang⁴ li² wu² ch'u⁴ pu⁴-k'an¹ hsing¹   7r
10. man³ mu⁴ yun² shan¹ hua⁴ nan² ch'eng²   7r
11. ch'üan² sheng¹ hsiang³ shih² tzu³-hsi⁴ t'ing¹   7r
12. chuan³ chüeh² ch'ai² men² ching⁴   5r

16: *Word by word*

1. Since/jump out/merit-fame/fire-pit,
2. Come/to/this/flower/moon/P'eng/Ying.
3. Keeping/this/good/field/several hundred/acres,
4. Watching/(for) a while/rain/ploughing/smoke/tilling.
5. At end/(in) heart/not alarmed,
6. Every/day/straight/sleep to/day break

96

7. Seeing/Hsieh-ch'uan/chickens/dogs/enjoy/peace.
8. Winding around/house/mulberry/hemp/green/smoke/rise.
9. Holding/cane/nowhere/cannot/walk.
10. Full/eyes/cloudy/hills/picture/difficult/complete.
11. Springs/sound/sounding/time/carefully/listen.
12. Turning/feel/thorn/gate/quiet.

16: *First draft*

Now that I've jumped out of the fire-pit of merit and fame,
I have come to this fairyland of flowers and moonlight.
Keeping several hundred acres of good land,
I watch for a while how it is tilled by rain and smoke.
In the end I no longer am alarmed,
And I can sleep till daybreak every day.
I can see at Hsieh-ch'uan chickens and dogs enjoying peace.
Around the house green smoke rises amongst mulberries and hemps.
Holding my cane, there is no place where I cannot enjoy my stroll.
Look where I will, I see clouds over the hills, and my painting cannot be finished.
When the sound of the springs starts, listen carefully.
Returning I feel so quiet within the thorn-gate.

16: *Note*

Hsieh-ch'uan, a small village in Kiangsi province, was once visited by the great poet of Chin, T'ao Yüan-ming, also known as T'ao Ch'ien. Hsieh-ch'uan usually suggests peace and quiet.

POEM 17: *Transliterated*

Author: Kuan Yun-shih
Title: 'Tai^4 jen^2 tso^4'
Tune: 'Sai^4-hung^2-ch'iu^1'

1. chan^4 hsi^1-feng^1 chi^3-tien^3 pin^1-hung^2 chih^4 8r
2. (kan^3 ch'i^3 wo^3) Nan^2-ch'ao^2 ch'ien^1 ku^3 shang^1-hsin^1 shih^4 7r
3. (chan^3 hua^1 chien^4) yü^4 hsieh^3 chi^3-chü^4 chih^1-hsin^1 shih^4 7r
4. (k'ung^1 chiao^1 wo^3)t'ing^2 shuang^1 hao^2 pan^4-hsiang^3 wu^2 ts'ai^{2}ssu^1 7r
5. wang^3-ch'ang^2 te^2-hsing^4 shih^2 5r
6. i^1-sao^3 wu^2 hsia^2-tz'u^1 5r
7. (chin^1-jih^4 ke^4) ping^4 yen^4-yen^4 3
8. (kang^1 hsieh^3 hsia^4) liang^3-ke^4 hsiang^1-ssu^1 tzu^4 5r

17: *Word by word*

1. Fighting/west/wind/several/dots/geese/come.
2. Aroused/me/Southern Dynasties/thousand years/heartbroken/events (affairs)

3. Spreading/flowery/pad/wish/to write/several words/knowing/heart (mind)/things.
4. In vain/makes/me/stop/brush/a while/have no/talented/thinking.
5. In past/got/mood/time
6. One/sweep/without/faults.
7. (But) today/sick/weary
8. Just/wrote/down/two/mutual/longing(love)/words

17: First draft

Fighting with the west wind, several visiting geese have come.
They remind me of the many heart-broken events of the southern dynasties.
Spreading out my writing pad, I wished to write a few lines of secret thoughts.
In vain, I could only lower my frost-coloured brush after a long while without any inspiration.
In the past when I was in the right mood,
I could sweep my brush without any fault.
But today, sick and weary
I can only put down two words—'mutual longing'.

POEM 18: *Transliterated*

Author: Teng Yü-pin
Title: 'Hsien² shih⁴'
Tune: 'Yen⁴-erh²-lo⁴ tai⁴ Te²-sheng⁴-ling⁴'

1.	ch'ien²-k'un¹ i¹ chuan⁴ wan²	5r
2.	jih⁴-yüeh⁴ shuang¹ fei¹ chien⁴	5r
3.	fu²-sheng¹ meng⁴ i¹-ch'ang²	5
4.	shih⁴-shih⁴ yun² ch'ien¹ pien⁴	5r
5.	wan⁴-li³ Yü⁴-men² Kuan¹	5
6.	ch'i¹ li³ tiao⁴-yü² t'an¹	5r
7.	hsiao³ jih⁴ Ch'ang²-an¹ chin⁴	5
8.	ch'iu¹-feng¹ Shu³-tao⁴ nan²	5r
9.	hsiu¹ kan¹	2r
10.	wu⁴-sha¹ ying¹-hsiung² han⁴	5r
11.	k'an⁴-k'an⁴	2r
12.	hsing¹-hsing¹ liang³ pin⁴ pan¹	5r

18: Word by word

1. Universe/one/rolling/ball
2. Sun/moon/two/flying/arrows.
3. Floating/life/dream/one
4. World/affairs/cloud/thousand/changes.
5. Ten thousand/miles/Yü-men/Pass.
6. Seven/miles/fishing/beach.

7. Morning/sun/Ch'ang-an/near.
8. Autumn/wind/Sze-ch'uan/road/difficult.
9. Never/mind,
10. Wasted/much/a hero/man
11. Look/look,
12. Star-like/two/temple/grey.

18: *First draft*

The universe is like a rolling ball.
Sun and moon are like two flying arrows.
The floating life is like a dream.
And world affairs are like the changeable clouds.
Ten thousand miles away is the Yü-men Pass.
Seven miles long is the fishing beach.
In the morning sun, Ch'ang-an is very near.
But in autumn's wind, the road to Sze-ch'uan is very difficult.
Never mind.
A heroic man has been wasted.
Look!
Star-like his two temples have turned white.

18: *Notes*

Seven miles refers to Yen Tzu-ling who declined the invitation of the Emperor Wu-ti of the Eastern Han dynasty to serve in the government. Tzu-ling preferred to fish from his own 'seven-mile beach'.

Sze-ch'uan is the modern name of the ancient Shu district in Western China. Chinese poets often incorporate the sentence, 'The road to Shu is difficult.' into their poems. Chang-an, the capital city of the T'ang dynasty, frequently is used in poetry to suggest ambition i.e. the quest for fame.

POEM 19: *Transliterated*

Author: Pai Pen
Title: None
Tune: 'Ying^1-wu^3-ch'ü^3'

1. nung^2-chia^1 ying^1-wu^3 chou^1 pien^1 chu^4 7r
2. Shih^4 ke^4 (pu^1) shih^4-tzu^4 yü^2-fu^4 6r
3. lang^4-hua^1 chung^1 i^1-yeh^4 pien^3-chou^1 7
4. shui^4-sha^1 chiang^1-nan^2 yen^1 yü^3 6r
5. chüeh^2 lai^2 shih^2 man^3 yen^3 ch'ing^1 shan^1 7
6. tou^1 sou^3 lü^4 suo^1 kui^1-ch'ü^4 6r
7. suan^4 ts'ung^2-ch'ien^2 ts'o^4 yüan^4 t'ien^1-kung^1 7
8. shen^4 yeh^3 yu^3 an^1-p'ai^2 wo^3 ch'u^4 7r

19: *Word by word*

1. My house/Parrot Islet/side/lives.
2. (It) is/not/know/character/fisherman.
3. Waves/inside/a/leaf/shallow/boat,
4. Sleep/soundly/River/south/smoke/rain.
5. Wake up/time/full/eyes/green/mountains.
6. Shake/green/grass-coat/return.
7. Figured/before/wrongly/blame/Lord Heaven,
8. Indeed/also/has/arrange/me/place.

19: *First draft*

My home dwells beside Parrot Islet.
I am but an illiterate fisherman.
Amongst the waves there is a leaf-like flat boat.
I sleep through the smoky rain south of the river.
When awake, I behold the green mountains.
Shaking my grass rain-coat I return home.
Indeed I was wrong in blaming the Lord of Heaven,
For He has arranged a place for me.

POEM 20: *Transliterated*

Author: Ma Chih-yüan
Title: 'Shan^1-shih^4 ch'ing^2-lan^2'
Tune: 'Lo^4-mei^2-feng^1'

1. Hua^1 ts'un^1 wai^4 3
2. ts'ao^3 tien^4 hsi^1 3r
3. hsiao^3 hsia^2 ming^2 yü^3 shou^1 t'ien^1 chi^4 7r
4. ssu^4-wei^2 shan^1 i^1-kan^1 ts'an^2-chao^4 li^3 8r
5. chin^3 p'ing^2-feng^1 yu^4 t'ien^1 p'u^1 ts'ui^4 7r

20: *Word by word*

1. Flowery/village/outside
2. Grass/inn/west,
3. Morning/clouds/clear/rain/collect/sky/clear.
4. Four/sides/mountains/one/pole/sunset/in.
5. Silk/screen/again/adds/greenness.

20: *First draft*

Outside the flowery village,
And west of the grassy inn,
The morning sun is bright, the rain is over, and the sky clear.
All around, the mountains are illumined in the setting sun.
On the silk screen another layer of green is being added.

POEM 21: *Transliterated*

Author: Yao Sui
Title: 'Ssu⁴-shih² ching³'
Tune: 'Po¹-pu¹-tuan⁴'

1. ts'ao³ ch'i¹-ch'i¹   3r
2. jih⁴ ch'ih²-ch'ih²   3r
3. wang²-sun¹ shih⁴-nü³ ch'un¹ yu²-hsi⁴   7r
4. kung¹-tien⁴ feng¹ wei¹ yen⁴ ch'üeh⁴ fei¹   7r
5. ch'ih² t'ang² sha¹ nuan³ yüan¹-yang¹ shui⁴   7r
6. cheng⁴ chih⁴-che¹ yang³ hua¹ t'ien¹-ch'i⁴   7r

21: *Word by word*

1. Grass/luxuriant
2. Sun/slow.
3. Young men/young ladies/spring/frolick.
4. Palaces/wind/gentle/swallows/sparrows/fly.
5. Pond/sand/warm/Mandarin ducks/sleep.
6. Just/encounters/raise/flowers/climate.

21: *First draft*

Green grows the grass.
Slowly moves the sun.
Young men and young girls are playing in the springtime.
In the palaces, the wind is gentle; swallows and sparrows are flying.
In the pond, the sand is warm, and mandarin ducks are sleeping there.
It is the right climate to raise flowers.

POEM 22: *Transliterated*

Author: Hsüeh Ang-fu
Title: None
Tune: 'Ch'u³-t'ien¹-yao² tai⁴ Ch'ing¹-chiang¹-yin³'

1. hua¹ k'ai¹ jen² cheng⁴ huan¹   5
2. hua¹ lo⁴ ch'un¹ ju² tsui⁴   5r
3. ch'un¹ tsui⁴ yu³-shih² hsing³   5
4. jen¹ lao³ huan¹ nan² hui⁴   5r
5. i¹-chiang¹ ch'un¹-shui³ liu²   5
6. wan⁴-tien³ yang²-hua¹ chui⁴   5r
7. shui²-tao⁴ shih⁴ yang²-hua¹   5
8. tien³-tien³ li²-jen² lei⁴   5r
9. hui²-shou³ yu³-ch'ing² feng¹ wan⁴-li³   7
10. miao³-miao³ t'ien¹ wu²-chi⁴   5r
11. ch'ou² kung⁴ hai³-ch'ao² lai²   5
12. ch'ao² ch'ü⁴ ch'ou² nan² t'ui⁴   5r
13. (keng⁴)na³-k'an¹ wan³ lai² feng¹ yu⁴ chi²   7r

22: *Word by word*

1. Flower/blooms/people/just/happy.
2. Flower/falls/spring/like/drunk.
3. Spring/drunk/some time/sobers (up).
4. Man/old/joy(happiness)/hard/to meet.
5. One/river/spring/water/flows,
6. Ten thousand/dots/willow/flower/fall.
7. Who/says/(it) is/willow's flower?
8. Dot/dot/departing/person's/tears.
9. Turn back/head/have/passion/wind/ten thousand/miles,
10. Distantly/heaven/has no/limit.
11. Sadness/with/sea/tide/come,
12. Tide/goes(away)/sadness/hard/to retreat.
13. Moreover/How/bear/evening/comes/wind/again/fierce?

22: *First Draft*

When flowers bloom, people are just joyous.
When flowers fall, spring is like a drunken person.
When spring is drunk, it sometimes grows sober.
But when a man becomes old, he cannot find happiness again.
A river, full of spring water, flows.
A thousand willow catkins fall.
Who says it is the flower of the willow?
Dot by dot, they are tears of someone departing.
Turning his head round, he is sentimental, but the wind blows ten thousand miles away.
No matter how you look, the sky has no limit.
Sadness came in with the tide.
The tide is gone; but sadness remains.
Moreover, how can I bear the fierceness of the evening wind?

POEM 23: *Transliterated*

Author: Hsüeh Ang-fu
Title: None
Tune: 'Chu'u³-t'ien¹-Yao² tai⁴ Ch'ing¹-chiang¹-yın³'

1.	yu³-i⁴ sung⁴ ch'un¹ kui¹	5
2.	wu²-chi⁴ liu² ch'un¹ chu⁴	5r
3.	ming²-nien² yu⁴ cho² lai²	5
4.	ho²-ssu⁴ hsiu¹ kui¹-ch'ü⁴	5r
5.	t'ao²-hua¹ yeh³ chieh³-ch'ou²	5
6.	tien³-tien³ p'iao¹ hung² yü⁴	5r
7.	mu⁴ tuan⁴ Ch'u³ t'ien¹ yao²	5
8.	pu¹-chien⁴ ch'un¹ kui¹ lu⁴	5r
9.	ch'un¹ jo⁴ yu³-ch'ing² ch'un¹ keng⁴ k'u³	7r
10.	an⁴ li³ shao³-kuang¹ tu⁴	5r

11. hsi¹-yang² shan¹ wai⁴ shan¹   5
12. ch'un¹ shui³ tu⁴ p'ang² tu⁴   5r
13. pu¹-chih¹ na³-ta¹-erh² (shih⁴) ch'un¹ ch'ü⁴-ch'u⁴ 7r

23: *Word by word*

1. Have/intentions/to send/spring back,
2. No/plan/retain/spring/stay.
3. Next year/again/will come,
4. How/like/not/return.
5. Peach/blossom/also/understand/sadness,
6. Point/point/float/red/jade.
7. Eyes/cut off(break)/Ch'u/sky/distant(remote),
8. Not/see/spring/returning/route(road).
9. Spring/if/has/feelings/spring/more/suffer,
10. In/secret/time/passes.
11. Sunset/mountain/outside(beyond)/mountains,
12. Spring/water/ferry/side/ferry.
13. Not/know/where(is)/spring's/dwelling place?

23: *First draft*

I intend to send back spring,
Having no means of keeping her here.
Since next year she will come again,
She might as well stay for good.
The peach blossom seems to understand my sadness,
For dot by dot it sends its red jade petals floating around.
My eyes stop at the remote sky of Ch'u,
But cannot find spring's return route.
If spring should have emotion, she would suffer more;
Imperceptibly her youth passes.
The sun sets behind the mountains beyond mountains.
The spring river flows by the ferry.
I don't know where spring's dwelling place is.

23: *Note*

Ch'u is a part of the southwestern section of China often regarded in literature as remote.

POEM 24: *Transliterated*

Author: Li Chih-yüan
Title: 'Mu⁴ ch'un¹'
Tune: 'Ying²-hsien¹-k'o⁴'

1. ch'ui¹ lo⁴ hung²   3r
2. tung⁴ hua¹ feng¹   3r
3. shen¹ yüan⁴ ch'ui²-yang² ch'ing¹ wu⁴ chung¹ 7r

4. hsiao³ ch'uang¹ hsien²	3
5. t'ing² hsiu⁴-kung¹	3r
6. lien²-mo⁴ ch'ung²-ch'ung²	4r
7. pu¹ so³ hsiang¹-ssu¹ meng⁴	5r

24: *Word by word*

1. Blow/fallen/red,
2. (The) tung-flower/wind.
3. Deep/courtyard/weeping-willow/light/fog/in,
4. Small/window/idle,
5. Stop/embroidery/work.
6. Screens/layer(by)layer,
7. Not/lock/mutual/longing/dream.

24: *First draft*

The wind of the tung-tree flower
Blows the fallen red flowers.
In the deep courtyard, a weeping willow weeps in a light fog.
The small window is idle,
I stop my embroidery work.
Though screens and curtains are many layers thick,
They cannot lock out my dreams of requited love.

POEM 25: *Transliterated*

Author: Liu Chih
Title: 'Sung⁴ pieh²'
Tune: 'Yen⁴-erh²-lo⁴ tai⁴ Te²-sheng⁴-ling⁴'

1. ho² feng¹ nao⁴ yen⁴ ying¹	5r
2. li⁴ jih⁴ ming² t'ao² hsing⁴	5r
3. Ch'ang²-chiang¹ i¹-hsien⁴ p'ing²	5r
4. mu⁴ yü³ ch'ien¹ shan¹ ching⁴	5r
5. tsai³ chiu³ sung⁴ chün¹ hsing²	5r
6. che¹ liu³ hsi⁴ li²-ch'ing²	5r
7. meng⁴ li³ ssu¹ Liang²-yüan²	5
8. hua¹ shih² pieh² Wei⁴-ch'eng²	5r
9. ch'ang² t'ing²	2r
10. chih³-ch'ih³ jen² ku¹-ling⁴	5r
11. ch'ou² t'ing¹	2r
12. Yang²-kuan¹ ti⁴-ssu⁴ sheng¹	5r

25: *Word by word*

1. Warm/wind/excites/swallows/orioles.
2. Beautiful/sun/brightens/peach/apricot.
3. (The) Long/River/one/line /smooth.

4. Evening/rain/thousand/mountains/quiet.
5. Carry/wine/send/you/go;
6. Break/willow/tie/departing/sentiment.
7. Dream/in/think/Liang's/Garden;
8. Flower(blossom)/time/leaves/Wei-ch'eng.
9. (The) Long/pavilion
10. One/foot/a person/lonely.
11. Sadly/listen,
12. (The) Yang-kuan/(the) fourth/sound(tune)

25: *First draft*

The warm wind has livened the swallows and orioles.
The lovely sun has brightened the peach and apricot blossoms.
The Long River is as smooth as thread.
The evening rain has quieted the thousand mountains.
Carrying wine I send you off.
I break a willow to express my parting sorrow.
In my dreams I am thinking of Liang Garden.
At blossom time, you are leaving the Wei-ch'eng city.
At the long pavilion,
One foot away, a person becomes very lonely.
Listen! How sadly
The Yang-kuan tune sounds the fourth time.

25: *Note*

Wei is the name of a city often referred to as suggesting a point of departure.

POEM 26: *Transliterated*

Author: Ma Chiu-kao
Title: 'Ling² Ch'iao¹ T'ai² huai²-ku³'
Tune: 'Sai⁴-hung¹-ch'iu¹'

1. Ling²-Ch'iao¹ T'ai² p'an⁴ Huang²-shan¹-p'u⁴   7r
2. (shih⁴) san¹ ch'ien¹ ko¹ wu³ wang² chia¹ ch'u⁴   7r
3. Wang⁴-fu¹ Shan¹ hsia⁴ Wu¹-chiang¹ tu⁴   7r
4. (shih⁴) pa¹ ch'ien¹ tzu³-ti⁴ ssu¹ hsiang¹ ch'ü⁴   7r
5. Chiang¹-tung¹ jih⁴ mu⁴ yun²   5
6. Wei⁴ pei³ ch'un¹-t'ien¹ shu⁴   5r
7. ch'ing¹ shan¹ T'ai⁴-pai² fen² ju² ku⁴   7r

26: *Word by word*

1. Ling-ch'iao/Terrace/side/Huang-shan-p'u,
2. Is/three/thousand/song/dance/lose/home/place.
3. Wang-fu/Mountain/below/Wu/River/ferry,

4. Is/Eight/thousand/soldiers/think/home/gone.
5. River/east/sun/sets/cloud,
6. Wei/north/spring/time/trees.
7. Blue/mountains/T'ai-po/tomb/as/before.

26: *First draft*

By the Ling-ch'iao Terrace, Huang-shan-p'u
Was the place where three thousand revellers lost their all.
The ferry of the Wu River below the Wang-fu Mountain,
Was the place where eight thousand soldiers left thinking of home.
East of the River, the clouds glow at sunset,
North of the Wei river, trees show spring time.
On the green hill Li Po's tomb is still the same.

26: *Note*

Li T'ai-Po was the great poet of the T'ang period.

POEM 27: *Transliterated*

Author: Ma Chiu-kao
Title: 'Chi² ku³'
Tune: 'Shui³-hsien¹-tzu³'

1. chi³-nien² wu²-shih⁴ p'ang² chiang¹ hu²	7r
2. tsui⁴ tao³ Huang²-kung¹ chiu⁴ chiu³-lu²	7r
3. jen²-chien¹ tsung⁴ yu³ shang¹-hsin¹ ch'u⁴	7r
4. yeh³ pu¹ tao⁴ Liu² Ling² feng² shang⁴ t'u³	8r
5. tsui⁴-hsiang¹ chung¹ pu¹ pien⁴ hsien² yü⁴	7r
6. tui⁴ feng¹-liu² jen²-wu⁴	5r
7. k'an⁴ chiang¹ shan¹ hua⁴-t'u²	5r
8. pu¹ tsui⁴ tao³ ho²-ju²	5r

27: *Word by Word*

1. Several/years/had/nothing/beside/rivers/lakes,
2. Drunk/fell/Lord/Huang's/old/wine/stove.
3. Human/world/though/there are/heartbroken/spots(things),
4. Also/not/arrive (at)/Liu Ling's/tomb/top/earth.
5. Drunk/land/in/not/distinguish/wise/foolish,
6. Facing/romantic/people,
7. Watch/river/mountain/pictures.
8. (If)not/drunk/what (then)?

27: *First draft*

For several years I did nothing but roamed along rivers and lakes.
I often became drunk by the old wine stove of Lord Huang.
In the human world, even though there are heartbreaking times

They would not come to the earth of Liu Ling's tomb.
In the land of the drunk the wise cannot be distinguished from the dumb.
Facing those romantic people,
Watching the pictures of rivers and mountains,
If I don't get drunk, what else is there?

27: Notes

Lord Huang's wine-stove, or cup, in Chinese literature, refers to wine drinking.

Liu Ling, associated with the 'Seven Virtues of the Bamboo Grove', during the Chin dynasty, was a great wine drinker. He wrote an essay entitled, 'Praising the Virtues of Wine'.

POEM 28: *Transliterated*

Author: Jen Yü
Title: 'Ho^2 yu^3-jen^2 yun^4'
Tune: 'Hung^2-hsiu^4-hsieh^2'

1. mao^2-wu^1 ch'iu^1-feng^1 ch'ui^1 p'o^4	6r
2. kui^4 ts'ung^1 yeh^4 yüeh^4 k'ung^1 kuo^4	6r
3. Huai^2-nan^2 chao^1 yin^3 ku^4 ch'ing^2 to^1	7r
4. wu^2 hsin^1 teng^1 hu^3-chang^4	5
5. yu^3 meng^4 tao^4 yü^2 so^1	5r
6. pu^1 kui^1-lai^2 teng^3 shen^2-mo^1	6r

28: *Word by word*

1. Grass/hut/autumn/wind/blow/through.
2. Cinnamon-tree/bushes/night/moon/in vain/passes.
3. Huai/south/summon/retirement/old/sentiments/much.
4. Without/interest/climb up/tiger/tent,
5. Have/dreams/to(reach)/fishing/grass-coat.
6. Not/return/wait for/what?

28: *First draft*

The grass hut was blown through by the autumn wind.
In the cinnamon bushes, the evening moon had passed in vain.
To the south of Huai I am lured by an old sentiment to retire.
Without wanting to climb up to the tiger's tent,
My dreams went to fishing in a grass rain-coat.
By not returning now, what am I waiting for?

28: *Note*

The *'Tiger's Tent'* refers to the headquarters of the commanding general of an army. By extension it suggests the seat of any high official.

POEM 29: *Transliterated*

Author: Jen Yü
Title: None
Tune: 'Ch'en[2]-tsui[4]-tung[1]-feng[1]'

1. yu[3]-tai[4] chiang[1]-shan[1] hsin[4] mei[3]   6r
2. wu[2]-ch'ing[2] sui[4]-yüeh[4] hsiang[1] ts'ui[1]   6r
3. tung[1] li[3] lai[2]   3
4. hsi[1] lin[2] tsui[4]   3r
5. t'ing[1] yü[2] ch'iao[2] chiang[3] hsieh[1] hsing[1] fei[4] 7r
6. i[1]-chiu[4] Chung[1]-yüan[2] i[1] pu[4]-i[1]   7
7. keng[4] hsiu[1]-hsiang[3] ch'i[2]-lin[2] hua[4] li[3] 7r

29: *Word by word*

1. Awaiting/rivers/mountains/indeed/beautiful.
2. Emotionless/years/months/are urging.
3. Eastern/neighbour/comes,
4. Western/neighbour/drunk.
5. Listen to/fisherman/woodsmen/(to) talk (about)/rises/falls.
6. Still/Central Plain's/cotton-clothed (man),
7. No longer/think/unicorn/picture/in.

29: *First draft*

The awaiting rivers and mountains are indeed beautiful.
But the ruthless years and months impel me.
The east neighbour comes.
The west neighbour is drunk.
Listen to the fisherman and woodsman talking about rises and falls.
I am still a plain-clothed man of the Central Plains.
I do not wish to be hung among the pictures of the Ch'i-lin Tower.

29: *Note*

Ch'i-lin Tower refers to the Palace of the Unicorn, built by the Emperor Hsüan-ti of Han, in which portraits of meritorious ministers and generals were hung.

POEM 30: *Transliterated*

Author: Ch'a Te-ch'ing
Title: 'Huai[2] ku[3]'
Tune: 'Che[1]-kui[4]-ling[4]'

1. wen[4] ts'ung[2]-lai[2] shui[2] shih[4] ying[1]-hsiung[2]   7r
2. i[1]-ke[4] nung[2]-fu[1]   4
3. i[1]-ke[4] yü[2]-weng[1]   4r
4. hui[3]-chi[4] Nan[2]-yang[2]   4
5. ch'i[1] shen[1] Tung[1]-hai[3]   4
6. i[1]-chü[3] ch'eng[2]-kung[1]   4r

7 pa¹-chen⁴-t'u² ming² ch'eng² Wo⁴-lung³	7r
8. liu⁴-t'ao¹-shu¹ kung¹ tsai⁴ Fei¹-hsiung²	7r
9. pa⁴-yeh⁴ ch'eng² k'ung¹	4r
10. i²-hen⁴ wu²-ch'iung²	4r
11. Shu³-tao⁴ han² yun²	4
12. Wei⁴-shui³ ch'iu¹-feng¹	4r

30: *Word by word*

1. Ask/hitherto/who/is/hero?
2. One/farmer,
3. One/fisherman.
4. Hide/traces/(at)Nan-yang.
5. Live/Tung-hai.
6. One/try(raise)/succeeded
7. Eight-front/strategy/name/established/Wo-Lung.
8. Six Tactics/books/merit/lies (with)/Fei-hsiung.
9. Hegemony/task/became/empty.
10. Regret/unlimited.
11. Shu/road/cold/clouds.
12. Wei/River/autumn/wind.

30: *First draft*

May I ask, who were the heroes so far?
One was a farmer,
The other was a fisherman.
One hid his traces at Nan-yang.
One lived in obscurity at Tung-hai.
But at one stroke, they succeeded.
The Eight-front strategy has established the name Wo-lung.
The Six Tactics Book praised Fei-hsiung.
But their attempts to rule were vain;
And their regrets were limitless.
The road to Shu is now covered with cold clouds.
And the Wei River is blown by the autumn wind.

30: *Notes*

'*Heroes of the Past*' tells the stories of Chu-ko Liang of the period of the Three Kingdoms, and Chiang Tzu-ya of the early Chou period. Before they became prominent, Chu-ko lived as a farmer on his estate at Nan-yang, and Chiang lived at Tung-hai. After their successes, Chu-ko was known as Wo-lung (meaning Resting Dragon), and Chiang as Fei-hsiung (meaning Flying Bear).

The strategy of Eight Fronts was that which Chu-ko Liang employed successfully in aiding the king of Shu.

Wo-lung is another name of Chu-ko Liang.

Fei-hsiung is another name of Lü Shang, also known as Chiang T'ai-kung, prime minister of King Wen of Chou (*c.* 1122 BC). Before being called to serve the Chou Court, Fei-hsiung lived, at his native home Tung-hai, the life of a fisherman.

The Shu road refers to the high mountain road, approaching the State of Shu.

The Wei River is reportedly the place where King Wen of Chou met with Lü Shang. It usually suggests the Chou Court, which controlled what is now Shensi Province and through which province the Wei River flows.

POEM 31: *Transliterated*

Author: Lu Chih
Title: None
Tune: 'Ch'en²-tsui⁴-tung¹-feng¹'

1. kua⁴ chüeh²-pi¹ k'u¹ shu¹ tao⁴ i³   7r
2. lo⁴ ts'an²-hsia² ku¹ wu⁴ ch'i² fei¹   7r
3. ssu⁴-wei² pu¹ chin⁴ shan¹   5
4. i¹ wang⁴ wu²-ch'iung² shui³   5r
5. san⁴ hsi¹-feng¹ man³ t'ien¹ ch'iu¹-i⁴   7r
6. yeh⁴ ching⁴ yun² fan¹ yüeh⁴-ying³ ti¹   7r
7. tsai³ wo³ tsai⁴ Hsiao¹ Hsiang¹ hua⁴ li³   7r

31: *Word by word*

1. Hanging/steep/wall(cliff)/withered/pine/upset/lean,
2. Fallen/remaining/clouds/lone/goose/together/fly.
3. Four/sides/no/limited/mountains,
4. One/look/without/finite/river.
5. Dispersed/west/wind/full/sky/autumn/idea.
6. Night/quiet/cloud/sail/moon/shadow/low,
7. Carry/me/at/Hsiao/Hsiang/picture/inside.

31: *First draft*

Clinging to a steep cliff a withered pine leans over.
A few low lingering clouds and a lone goose are flying together.
On all sides are mountains without limit.
With one glance I see the infinite river.
A west wind disperses the autumn scene all over the sky.
The night is quiet, the sail-like cloud and the moon shadow are low.
They carry me into the picture of Hsiao and Hsiang rivers.

POEM 32: *Transliterated*

Author: Ma Chih-yüan
Title: None
Tune: 'Ssu⁴-k'uai⁴-yü⁴'

1. chiu³ hsüan² ku¹   3
2. yü² hsin¹ mai³   3r

3. man³ yen³ yun¹ shan¹ hua⁴-t'u² k'ai¹   7r
4. ch'ing¹-feng¹ ming²-yüeh⁴ huan² shih¹-chai⁴   7r
5. pen³ shih⁴ ke⁴ lan³-san³ jen²   6
6. yu⁴ wu² shen⁴ ching¹-chi⁴ ts'ai²   6r
7. kui¹-ch'ü⁴ lai²   3r

32: *Word by word*

1. Wine/just/bought,
2. Fish/newly/purchased.
3. Full/eyes/clouds/mountains/picture/opens up.
4. Pure/wind/bright/moon/repay/poet/debt.
5. Basically/am/lazy/undisciplined/man,
6. Again/without/any/administration/talent.
7. Return/come.

32: *First draft*

With wine just bought,
And fish newly purchased,
An eyeful of pictures of clouds and mountains are spreading out.
Pure wind and bright moon have paid my poetic debt.
I am basically a lazy and undisciplined man,
And without any talent for administration,
I'll go back.

POEM 33: *Transliterated*

Author: Ma Chih-yüan
Title: None
Tune: 'Po¹-pu¹-tuan⁴'

1. pu⁴-i¹ chung¹   3r
2. wen⁴ ying¹-hsiung²   3r
3. wang² t'u² pa⁴-yeh⁴ ch'eng² ho² yung⁴   7r
4. ho²-shu³ kao¹-ti¹ liu⁴-tai⁴ kung¹   7r
5. ch'iu¹-wu² yüan³-chin⁴ ch'ien¹ kuan¹ chiung³   7r
6. i¹-ch'ang² e⁴-meng⁴   4r

33: *Word by word*

1. Cotton/clothes/in,
2. Ask/heroes.
3. King/attempts/hegemony/career(task)/fulfil/what/purpose?
4. Grain/millets/high/low/six/dynasties/palaces.
5. Wu-t'ung(trees)/far/near/thousand/officials/tombs.
6. One/big/bad/dream.

33: *First draft*

In my plain clothes,
I ask the heroes:
For what purpose did the kings attempt their careers of hegemony?
The grain and millets are grown high and low in the old palaces of the six dynasties.
And the wu-t'ung trees are far and near around a thousand officials' tombs.
It is merely a nightmare!

33: *Note*

Wu-t'ung trees are usually associated with autumn.

POEM 34: *Transliterated*

Author: Chang K'e-chiu
Title: 'Ch'un¹ ch'ou²'
Tune: 'Ssu⁴-k'uai⁴-yü⁴'

1. hsiao³ meng⁴ yun²	3r
2. ts'an² chuang¹ fen³	3r
3. i¹-tien³ fang¹-hsin¹ yüan⁴ wang²-sun¹	7r
4. shih² nien² pu¹ chi⁴ p'ing²-an¹ hsin⁴	7r
5. lü⁴ shui³ pin¹	3r
6. pi⁴ ts'ao³ ch'un¹	3r
7. hung² hsing⁴ ts'un¹	3r

34: *Word by word*

1. Morning/dream/cloud,
2. Remaining/make-up/rouge.
3. A (little)bit(of)/tender(sweet)/heart(mind)/blame/(my)young man.
4. Ten/years/not/sent/peace/letters.
5. Green/river/bank,
6. Blue/grass/spring,
7. Red/apricot/village.

34: *First draft*

My morning dream is like cloud.
My make-up rouge has faded away.
In my tiny fragile heart I blame my love.
For ten years, he has not sent any letter of peace.
By the side of green waters,
In spring of blue grass,
At a village of red apricot.

POEM 35: *Transliterated*

Author: Chang K'e-chiu
Title: 'Ch'iu¹ ssu¹'
Tune: 'Shui³-hsien¹-tzu³'

1. t'ien¹-pien¹ pai²-yen⁴ hsieh³ han² yun²   7r
2. ching⁴ li³ ch'ing¹-luan² shou⁴ yü⁴-jen²   7r
3. ch'iu¹-feng¹ tso²-yeh⁴ ch'ou² ch'eng² chen⁴   7r
4. ssu¹ chün¹ pu¹ chien⁴ chün¹   5r
5. huan³ ko¹ tu²-tzu⁴ k'ai¹ tsun¹   6r
6. teng¹ t'iao¹ chin⁴   3r
7. chiu³ pan⁴ hsün¹   3r
8. ju²-tz'u³ huang²-hun¹   4r

35: *Word by word*

1. Heaven(sky)/edge/white/geese/write/cold/clouds.
2. Mirror/inside/green/phoenix/lean/jade/person.
3. Autumn/wind/last night/sadness/became/showers(gust).
4. Think/you/not/seeing/you.
5. Slow/song/alone/open/wine/jug.
6. Lamp/plucked/through,
7. Wine/half/drunk,
8. Such/evening.

35: *First draft*

At the edge of heaven white geese are writing in the cold clouds.
Seen in the mirror the green phoenix and the jade figure are thin.
Last night the autumn wind and my sadness tangled into a gust.
I thought of you, but I could not see you.
So with a slow song I took up the wine jug.
The wick in the lamp was trimmed to the end.
And I was half drunk with wine.
Such was the evening!

POEM 36: *Transliterated*

Author: Hsü Tsai-ssu
Title: None
Tune: 'Hung²-chin³-p'ao²'

1. (na⁴ lao³ tzu³) ai⁴ ch'ing¹-hsien² chu²-i⁴ pieh²   6r
2. tiao⁴ T'ung²-chiang¹ chiang¹ shang⁴ hsüeh³   6r
3. fan⁴ T'ung²-chiang¹ chiang¹ shang⁴ yüeh⁴   6r
4. chün¹-wang² hsiang³-nien⁴ che³   5r
5. hsüan¹ tao⁴ feng⁴-huang²-ch'üeh⁴   5r
6. hsiang³-che¹ ch'i¹ li³ yü² t'an¹   6
7. chiang¹-che¹ i¹ kou¹ hsiang³ erh³   6
8. (wang⁴-che¹) Fu⁴-ch'un¹-shan¹ kui¹ ch'ü⁴ yeh³   6r

36: *Word by word*

1. That/old/man/love/leisure/ideas/different,
2. Fishing/T'ung river/river/on/snow.
3. Sailing/T'ung river/river/on/moon.
4. King/think(of)/him.
5. Summon/to/Phoenix/palaces.
6. Think(of)/seven/miles/fishing/beach,
7. Holding/a hook/fragrant/bait,
8. Looking/at/Fu-ch'un Mountain/return/oh!

36: *First draft*

That old man who loved leisure had strange ideas
Fishing in the snow on the T'ung River,
Sailing in the moonlight on the T'ung River.
The King, thinking of him,
Summoned him to his phoenix-palaces.
Thinking of the seven-mile long fishing beach,
He took a hook-full of bait,
Looking at the Fu-ch'un Mountain, he went back.

36: *Note*

Fu-ch'un refers to Mount Fu-ch'un to which Yen Tzu-ling, originally from Eastern Han, retired from public life.

POEM 37: *Transliterated*

Author: Chang K'e-chiu
Title: 'Ch'un^1 yeh^4'
Tune: 'Hung^2-hsiu^4-hsieh^2'

1. yen^4-tzu^3 lai^2 shih^2 ping^4 chiu^3	6
2. mu^3-tan^1 k'ai^1 ch'u^4 shih^1 ch'ing^2	6r
3. t'ing^2-yüan^4 huang^2-hun^1 yü^3 ch'u^1 ch'ing^2	7r
4. ching^4 hsin^1 hsien^2 kua^4 yüeh^4	5
5. cheng^1 shou^3 sui^4 t'an^2 ping^1	5r
6. tsun^1 ch'ien^2 ch'un^1 yeh^4 yung^3	5r

37: *Word by word*

1. Swallow/came/time/sick/wine,
2. Peony/bloom/place/poetic/sentiment.
3. Courtyard/evening/rain/just/clear.
4. Mirror/heart(centre)/leisurely/hang/moon.
5. Zither/hand/crush/pluck/ice.
6. Jug/front/spring/night/long.

37: *First draft*

When the swallows came, I was sick on wine.
Where the peony bloomed, I was aroused to poetry.
In the courtyard, at evening time, rain was just over.
In the centre of the mirror the moon was hanging idly.
My zither hand smashed and broke the ice.
By the wine jug, the spring night was long.

POEM 38: *Transliterated*

Author: Chang K'e-chiu
Title: 'Ch'un¹ ssu¹'
Tune: 'Ch'ao²-t'ien¹-tzu³'

1. ling²-hua¹ p'o⁴ liang³ pien¹   5r
2. yao² ch'in² tuan⁴ ssu⁴ hsüan²   5r
3. en¹ yu⁴ fan¹ ch'eng² yüan⁴   5r
4. huang² yun² ku¹ yen⁴ t'ui⁴ hua¹ tien⁴   7r
5. hsiu¹ yen³ shuang¹ luan² shan⁴   5r
6. kui¹ yen⁴ nien²-nien²   4r
7. li²-hen⁴ mien²-mien²   4r
8. yu⁴ Hsi¹-hu² pai⁴ sao³ t'ien¹   6r
9. ssu⁴ ch'ien²   2r
10. shang⁴ ch'uan²   2r
11. shih⁴ chao⁴ wo³ shang¹ ch'un¹ mien⁴   6r

38: *Word by word*

1. Mirror/broke/both/sides,
2. Jade/lute/broke/four/strings,
3. Gratitude/again/became/hate.
4. Yellow/clouds/lone/goose/faded/flower/hairpin.
5. Bashful/cover up/both(pair)/phoenix/fan.
6. Returning/swallows/year/year.
7. Departing sorrow/linger/linger.
8. Again/West/Lake/bowing/sweeping/days.
9. Temple/front,
10. Board/boat,
11. Try/reflect/my/hurt/spring/face.

38: *First draft*

The mirror was broken in two.
And my jade lute broke four strings.
Love had become hate.
In the yellow clouds was a lone goose. My flower hairpins were down.
Bashfully I covered my face with a phoenix-patterned fan.

Though swallows come back year after year,
This departing sorrow of mine still lingers.
It is again time to pay tribute to ancestors' tombs.
In front of a temple,
I boarded a boat.
I tried to take a look at my spring-hurt face.

POEM 39: *Transliterated*

Author: Chang K'e-chiu
Title: 'Ch'iu¹ huai²'
Tune: 'Ch'ing¹-chiang¹-yin³'

1. hsi¹-feng¹ hsin⁴ lai² chia¹ wan⁴-li³	7r
2. wen⁴ wo³ kui¹-ch'i¹ wei⁴	5r
3. yen⁴ t'i² hung²-yeh⁴ t'ien¹	5
4. jen² tsui⁴ huang² hua¹ ti⁴	5r
5. pa¹-chiao¹ yü³ sheng¹ ch'iu¹ meng⁴ li³	7r

39: *Word by word*
1. West/wind/letter/came/home/ten/thousand/miles.
2. Ask/my/returning/date/not.
3. Geese/chirp/red/leaves/sky.
4. Men/drunk/yellow/flowers/ground.
5. Banana/rain/sound/autumn/dream/inside.

39: *First draft*
The letter came with the west wind; my home is ten thousand miles away.
They asked me whether my returning date is set.
Wild geese cry in a sky red like autumn leaves.
Men become drunk in the yellow flower field.
Rain falling on banana leaves evokes an autumn dream.

POEM 40: *Transliterated*

Author: Chang K'e-chiu
Title: 'Ch'iu¹ huai²'
Tune: 'P'u³-t'ien¹-lo⁴'

1. wei⁴ shui² mang²	3
2. mo⁴-fei¹ ming⁴	3r
3. hsi¹-feng¹ i⁴ ma³	4
4. lo⁴ yüeh⁴ shu¹ teng¹	4r
5. ch'ing¹ t'ien¹ Shu³-tao⁴ nan²	5

6. hung² yeh⁴ Wu¹-chiang¹ leng³   5r
7. liang³ tzu⁴ kung¹-ming² p'in² k'an⁴ ching⁴   7r
8. pu⁴ jao² jen² pai²-fa³ hsing¹-hsing¹   7r
9. tiao⁴-yü² Tzu³-ling²   4r
10. ssu¹ ch'uan² Chi⁴-ying¹   4r
11. hsiao⁴ wo³ p'iao¹-ling²   4r

40: *Word by word*

1. For/whom/busy?
2. Is/not/fate?
3. West/wind/inn/horse,
4. Descending/moon/books/lamp.
5. Blue/sky/Shu/road/hard.
6. Red/leaves/Wu/River/cold.
7. Two/words/merit/fame/often/look at/mirror.
8. Not/let go/people/white/hair/star-star.
9. Fishing/Tzu-ling.
10. Thinking/wild vegetable/Chi-ying.
11. Laugh at/me/floating(wandering)/alone.

40: *First draft*

For whom am I so busy?
Could it be fate?
In the west wind, a horse in an inn,
In the descending moon, books and lamp.
Up in the blue sky, the road to Shu is indeed hard.
Among red leaves, the Wu River is cold.
For the two words—merit and fame—I look into the mirror often.
The star-like white hair would not let a man go.
Tzu-ling, who fished
And Chi-ying who was longing for his native vegetable,
Would laugh at my wandering so pitifully.

40: *Note*

Chi-ying was also known as Chang Han of the Chin dynasty. Chi-ying, a native of Wu, serving at Lo-yang, the Capital of Chin, was reminded one day when the autumn winds began to blow of the wild vegetables native to his own home town. He became so homesick as a result that he resigned his position and returned to his home.

POEM 41: *Transliterated*

Author: Chi'iao Chi
Title: 'Yu² Yüeh⁴ Fu²-wang²-fu³'
Tune: 'Shui³-hsien¹-tzu³'

1. sheng¹ ko¹ meng⁴ tuan⁴ chi²-li² sha¹ 7r
2. lo³ i³ hsiang¹ yü² yeh³ ts'ai⁴ hua¹ 7r
3. luan⁴ yun² lao³ shu⁴ hsi¹-yang² hsia⁴ 7r
4. yen⁴ hsiu¹ hsün² Wang² Hsieh⁴ chia¹ 6r
5. hen⁴ hsing¹ wang² nu⁴-sha⁴ (hsieh¹) ming² wa¹ 7r
6. p'u¹ chin³ ch'ih² mai² huang¹ wa³ 6r
7. liu² pei¹ t'ing² tui¹ p'o⁴ wa³ 6r
8. ho²-ch'u⁴ (yeh³) fan²-hua² 4r

41: *Word by word*
1. Flute/song/dream/broke/thorny/sand(beach).
2. Silk/fragrance/remains/wild/vegetable/flowers.
3. Disorderly/clouds/old/tree/sunset/below.
4. Swallows/don't/seek/Wang's/Hsieh's/houses.
5. Hate/rises/falls/angry/some/crowing/frogs
6. Spread/silk/pond/bury/barren/well wall.
7. Running/cup/pavilion/pile/broken/tiles.
8. Where/prosperous?

41: *First draft*
The flute songs and my dreams are all broken in the thorny beach.
The fragrance of silk remains with wild vegetables and flowers.
Disorderly clouds and an aged tree are under a setting sun.
Swallows, don't look for the houses of the Wangs and Hsiehs.
Hate rises and falls, angers some singing frogs
In the silken covered pond, the walls of a well are buried.
In the cup-flowing pavilion, broken tiles are piled up.
Where is the prosperous place?

POEM 42: *Transliterated*

Author: Ch'iao Chi
Title: 'Ping³-tzu³ yu² Yüeh⁴ huai² ku³'
Tune: 'Che¹-kui⁴-ling⁴'

1. P'eng²-lai² lao³ shu⁴ ts'ang¹ yun² 6r
2. ho²-shu³ kao¹-ti¹ 4
3. hu² t'u⁴ fen¹-yun² 4r
4. pan⁴ che¹ ts'an² pei¹ 4
5. k'ung¹ yü² ku⁴ chih³ 4
6. tsung³ shih⁴ huang² ch'en² 4r
7. Tung¹-Chin⁴ wang² yeh³ 4
8. tsai⁴ nan² hsün² ke⁴ Yu⁴-chün¹ 6r
9. Hsi¹-shih¹ ch'ü² yeh³ 4
10. chüeh² pu¹ chien⁴ shen⁴ chia¹-jen² 6r

11. hai³ ch'i⁴ ch'ang² hun¹   4r
12. t'i² chüeh² sheng¹ kan¹   4
13. t'ien¹-ti⁴ wu² ch'un¹   4r

42: *Word by word*

1. P'eng-lai/old/tree/green/clouds,
2. Grain/millet/high/low,
3. Fox/hare/crowded(plenty),
4. Half/broken/remaining/monument.
5. Vainly/remained/old/site.
6. Always/is/yellow/dust.
7. Eastern/Chin(Dynasty)/perished.
8. Again/hard/to find/a/Yu-chün.
9. Hsi-shih/gone.
10. Definitely/not/seen/any/beauties.
11. Sea/air/often(always)/gloom(hazy).
12. Chirping/cuckoo/voice(sound)/dry.
13. Heaven/earth/no/Spring.

42: *First draft*

At P'eng-lai, with its old trees and green clouds,
Grain and millets are grown high and low.
Foxes and hares are running around.
With but a half broken stone monument,
The site was left there empty.
It is nothing but yellow dust.
The Eastern Chin perished.
It is difficult to find another Yu-chün.
Hsi-shih has gone,
No longer can be found another beauty.
The sea air always appears hazy,
And the chirping cuckoo's voice becomes tedious.
No spring is seen in heaven or on earth.

42: *Notes*

Yu-chün refers to Wang Hsi-chih, respectfully called Yu-chün (Right Army), because he once served the Chin Court under the title of 'General of the Right Army'.

Hsi-shih was a famous beauty who lived during the period of the Warring States. During that time the two states, Wu and Yüeh, contended for supremacy over the remains of the Chou dynasty. Having been defeated in battle by Wu, the king of Yüeh, seeking revenge, presented one of his consorts, Hsi-shih, to the king of Wu. The king of Wu, overwhelmed by her beauty, lost interest in fighting Yüeh. The forces of Yüeh finally defeated those of Wu.

POEM 43: *Transliterated*

Author: Wang Yun
Title: None
Tune: 'Hsiao³-t'ao²-hung²'

1. ts'ai³ lien² jen² yü³ ke¹ ch'iu¹ yen¹	7r
2. p'o¹ ching⁴ ju² heng² lien⁴	5r
3. ju⁴ shou³ feng¹-kuang¹ mo⁴ liu² chuan³	7r
4. kung⁴ liu²-lien²	3r
5. hua⁴ ch'uan² i¹ hsiao⁴ ch'un¹-feng¹ mien⁴	7r
6. chiang¹ shan¹ hsin⁴ mei³	4
7. chung¹ fei¹ wo² t'u³	4
8. ho² jih⁴ shih⁴ kui¹ nien²	5r

43: *Word by word*
1. Plucking/lotus/person/words/separated(by)/autumn/smoke.
2. Waves/quiet/like/horizontal/thread(line).
3. Entering/hand/wind/light/don't/flow/turn.
4. Together/stay/linger.
5. Painted/boat/one/smile/spring/wind/face.
6. Rivers/mountains/indeed/beautiful.
7. After all/not/my/land.
8. What/day/is/return/(time)year?

43: *First draft*

The words of the lotus plucker are separated by the smokes in Autumn.
The waves are as quiet as a horizontal thread.
The elements we touch with our hands, don't flow away.
Together let's stay a while.
In a painted boat, a smile is registered on a face in the spring breeze.
The landscape is indeed beautiful.
But this is not my land.
When is my year for returning?

POEM 44: *Transliterated*

Author: Kuan Yun-shih
Title: None
Tune: 'Tien⁴-ch'ien²-huan¹'

1. ke¹ lien² t'ing¹	3r
2. chi³ fan¹ feng¹ sung⁴ mai⁴ hua¹ sheng¹	7r
3. yeh⁴ lai² wei¹ yü³ t'ien¹ chieh¹ ching⁴	7r
4. hsiao³ yüan⁴ hsien² t'ing²	4r
5. ch'ing¹ han² ts'ui⁴ hsiu⁴ sheng¹	5r

6. ch'uan¹ fang¹ ching⁴	3r
7. shih²-erh⁴ lan²-kan¹ p'ing²	5r
8. hsing⁴-hua¹ shu¹ ying³	4r
9. yang²-liu³ hsin¹ ch'ing²	4r

44: *Word by word*

1. Separated(by)/screen/listen,
2. Several/times/wind/sends/selling/flower/sound.
3. Night/came/a little/rain/sky/steps/quiet.
4. Small/courtyard/idle/garden.
5. Light/cold/green/sleeves/rise(come).
6. Through/fragrant/path,
7. Twelve/banisters/lean on.
8. Apricot/blossom/thin/shadow,
9. Willow/new(fresh)/sentiment.

44: *First draft*

Separated by the screen, I listen,
Frequently the wind sends in the flower pedlar's voice.
After the light rain of last night the sky and steps are quiet.
In a tiny yard and idle garden,
A light cold grows in my green sleeves.
Going through the flower path,
I lean on those twelve banisters.
The thin shadow of the apricot blossom,
And the willows have aroused fresh emotions.

POEM 45: *Transliterated*

Author: Anonymous
Title: None
Tune: 'Ch'ing¹-chiang¹-yin³'

1. lou² t'ou² liu³ ssu¹ feng¹ li⁴ juan³	7r
2. chi²-mo⁴ hsien² t'ing²-yüan⁴	5r
3. tu²-tzu⁴ i³ lan²-kan¹	5r
4. lo⁴ chin⁴ t'ao²-hua¹ p'ien⁴	5r
5. ch'ing¹ shan¹ pu⁴-chih¹ lang² chin⁴ yüan³	7r

45: *Word by word*

1. Tower/top/willow/threads/wind/strength/soft.
2. Lonely/idle/courtyard.
3. Alone/leaning against/banisters.
4. Fall/all/peach/blossom/petals.
5. Green/mountains/not/know/husband(lover)/near/far.

45: *First draft*

On the top of the tower, the willow branches are soft in the wind.
Lonely is the idle courtyard.
Alone I lean against the banisters.
The petals of the peach blossom have all fallen.
Over the green mountains, I do not know whether my lover is near or far.

POEM 46: *Transliterated*

Author: Sun Chou-ch'ing
Title: 'Ts'ai3-ch'a2 ko1'
Tune: 'Ma4-yü4-lang2 tai4 Kan3-huang2-en1'

1. ch'iu1-ch'ien1 yüan4-yü3 ch'un1 chiang1 mu4	7r
2. hung2 ti1 mi2	3
3. lü4 jung2 chu1	3r
4. chao1 yun2 ke1-tuan4 Yang2-t'ai2 lu4	7r
5. ch'ü4 feng4 ku1	3r
6. lai2 yen4 shu1	3r
7. liu2 ying1 tu4	3r
8. lan3 pu4 chieh1-ch'u2	4r
9. chüan4 li4 t'ing2-yü4	4r
10. ts'ao3 yen1 p'u1	3r
11. li2 hsüeh3 wu3	3r
12. liu3 feng1 fu2	3r
13. hua1 ching1 wo3 chü4	4r
14. wo3 ai4 hua1 yü2	4r
15. yü4-ou1 shu1	3r
16. chin1 ts'ui4 yü3	3r
17. pao3 hsiang1 chu1	3r
18. hsiu4 lo2 ju2	3r
19. chin3-chan4 shu1	3r
20. tang1-shih2 feng1 mi2 tao4 ts'eng2 wu2	7r
21. ch'ü1-chih3 kui1-ch'i1 k'ung1 tzu4 shu3	7r
22. i3-lan2 wu2 yü3 man4 ch'ou2-ch'u2	7r

46: *Word by word*

1. (The) swing/courtyard/spring/will/end(evening)
2. (The) red/shed/tears,
3. (The) green/smears/rouge.
4. (The) morning/clouds/cut off/Yang-t'ai/road.
5. (The) leaving/phoenix/alone,

6. (The) coming/swallow/sparse,
7. (The) flying/oriole/jealous.

8. (In)lazy/pace/courtyard/steps,
9. Tired/stand/tower's/corner.
10. Grass/smoke/spreads,
11. Pear/snow/dances,
12. Willow/wind/supports.
13. Flowers/startled/I/fear,
14. I/like/flower/lean.
15. Jade/dresser/comb,
16. Gold/jade/wings,
17. Precious/fragrant/pearls.

18. Embroider/silk/dress,
19. Silk/pad/letter.
20. That/time/sealed/tears/come/(or)not?
21. Bending/fingers/return/date/in vain/self/count.
22. Leaning/banister/without/words/slowly/hesitate.

46: *First draft*

With a swing in the courtyard, spring comes to an end.
The red sheds tears,
The green smears its rouge.
The morning clouds have obscured the road to Yang-t'ai.
The dying phoenix is alone,
The coming swallows are sparse,
The drifting oriole is jealous.

Lazily I pace down the steps.
Tired, I stand by the tower's corner.
The smoke of grass spreads,
The snowy pear-blossom dances,
The wind offers the willow its support.
The flowers are startled to see me so thin.
I am glad that flowers become fat.
My jade dresser's comb,
Gold and jade winged hair,
And precious fragrant pearls.

Embroider my silk dress,
And write on the silk tablet.
Has the letter sealed with tears come yet?
Bending my fingers I try to work out the day of his return.
Silently, leaning against the banister, I hesitate.

POEM 47: *Transliterated*

Author: Chung Ssu-ch'eng
Title: 'Ch'un¹'
Tune: 'Ma⁴-yü⁴-lang² tai⁴ Kan³-huang²-en¹ Ts'ai³-ch'a²-ko¹'

1. mei²-hua¹ lou⁴-hsieh⁴ yang²-ho² hsin¹	7r
2. ts'ai² ts'an² la⁴	3
3. yu⁴ hsin¹-ch'un¹	3r
4. tung¹-feng¹ pei³-an⁴ ping¹ hsiao¹ chin⁴	7r
5. Yüan²-yeh⁴ kuo⁴	3
6. She⁴-jih⁴ lin²	3r
7. Chung¹-ho² chin⁴	3r
8. t'ien¹-ch'i⁴ yin¹-wen¹	4r
9. hua¹ liu³ ching¹-shen²	4r
10. chia⁴ hsiang¹-lun²	3r
11. ch'ih⁴ yü⁴-le¹	3
12. tsui⁴ yu²-jen²	3r
13. ch'ing¹-ming² kuo⁴-liao³	4
14. fei¹ hsü⁴ fen¹-fen¹	4r
15. ke¹ ku¹ ts'un¹	3r
16. wen² tu⁴-yü³	3
17. yüan⁴ Tung¹-chün²	3r
18. t'an⁴ fang¹ ch'en²	3r
19. i³ san¹-fen¹	3r
20. erh⁴-fen¹ liu²-shui³ i¹-fen¹ ch'en²	7r
21. chi⁴-chi⁴ lo⁴-hua¹ shang¹ mu⁴ ching³	7r
22. ch'i¹-ch'i¹ fang¹-ts'ao³ p'a⁴ huang²-hun¹	7r

47: *Word by word*

1. Plum/flower/revealed/sun/warm/message.
2. Just/faded/wax (month),
3. Again/new/spring.
4. East/wind/north/shore/ice/melted away.
5. New Year's/night/over(passed),
6. Festival/Day/at hand.
7. Mid-spring/near.

8. Weather/warm
9. Flower/willow/spirit.
10. Drive/fragrant/wheels,
11. Gallop/jade/reins,
12. Drunken/roaming/people.

13. Spring-festival/passed,
14. Flying/catkins/profused.
15. Separated(by)/lone/village,
16. Heard/cuckoo,
17. Complain/East/Lord.

18. Sigh(for)/beautiful/days,
19. Already/three/divided.
20. Two/parts/flowing/water/one/part/dust.
21. Quietly/fallen/flowers/hurt/evening/scenery.
22. Moistened/fragrant/grass/fear/evening.

47: *First draft*

The plum blossom has revealed the sunny, warm message.
Just over the winter month,
It is New Year again.
The East wind has melted the ice on the northern shore.
New Year's eve has passed,
The Village Day is coming.
And mid-spring is drawing to a close.

The weather is warm,
Both flower and willow are in good spirits.
Driving their fragrant carriage,
Holding the jade reins,
The sight-seers are intoxicated.
The Spring Festival is just over,
Catkins are flying everywhere.
Separated by a lone village,
Hearing a cuckoo bird,
I begin to complain about the East Lord.

Lament over the beautiful days,
Already divided into three-parts.
Two parts are the running river, and one part the dust.
Quiet are the fallen flowers that are hurt by the evening scene.
The moistened fragrant grass is worried about the evening.

SONG CHAIN I

Author: Kuan Han-ch'ing
Title: 'Kui^1 yüan^4'

POEM 48A: *Transliterated*

Tune: 'Ts'ui^4-ch'ün^2-yao^1'

1. hsiao^3-lai^2 yü^3 kuo^4 shan^1 heng^2 hsiu^4 7r
2. yeh^3 shui^3 chang^4 ting^1-chou^1 5r

3. lan²-kan¹ i³ pien⁴ k'ung¹ hui²-shou³   7r
4. hsia⁴ wei¹ lou²   3r
5. i¹ t'ien¹ feng¹ wu⁴ mu⁴ shang¹ ch'iu¹   7r

48A: *Word by word*

1. Morning/came/rain/passed/mountain/appears(horizontally)/elegance.
2. Wild/water/swollen/islets.
3. Banisters/lean/through/in vain/turn/head.
4. Going down/dangerous/tower,
5. One/day(heaven, sky)/wind/things/late(evening)/hurt/autumn.

48A: *First draft*

When morning came, rain was over, the hills present elegance.
Wild water has swollen the islets.
After having leaned against the banisters, I turn my head in vain.
Coming down the dangerous tower,
I see everything under the sky feels hurt by the late autumn.

POEM 48B: *Transliterated*

B—*Tune:* 'Liu⁴-yao¹-pien⁴'

1. cha⁴ liang² shih²-hou⁴   4r
2. hsi¹-feng¹ t'ou⁴   3r
3. pi⁴ wu² t'o¹ yeh⁴   4
4. yü² shu³ ts'ai² shou¹   4r
5. hsiang¹ sheng¹ feng⁴ k'ou³   4r
6. lien² ch'ui² yü⁴ kou¹   4r
7. hsiao³ yüan⁴ shen¹ hsien² ch'ing¹ chou⁴   6r
8. ch'ing¹ yu¹   2r
9. t'ing¹ sheng¹-sheng¹ ch'an² tsao⁴ liu³ shao¹ t'ou²   8r

48B: *Word by word*

1. Just/chilly/time.
2. West/wind/penetrates.
3. Green/wu-t'ung(tree)/fell/leaves.
4. Remaining/summer/just/collected(withdrawn).
5. Fragrance/grows/phoenix/mouth.
6. Screen/hangs/jade/hook.
7. Small/courtyard/deep/idle/bright/daylight.
8. Pure/quiet,
9. Hear/sound-sound/cicada/cries/willow/branch/end.

48B: *First draft*

It is just the chilly time.
The west wind is penetrating.
Leaves fall from the wu-t'ung tree.

The remaining summer is just folded.
Fragrance grows at the mouth of the phoenix(burner).
The screen is hanging on a jade hook.
The tiny courtyard is deep and idle in broad daylight,
Pure and quiet.
Listen to the every cry of the cicada at the end of the willow branch.

POEM 48C: *Transliterated*

Tune: 'Chi⁴ sheng¹-ts'ao³'

1. wei⁴-shen⁴ yu¹	3r
2. wei⁴-shen⁴ ch'ou²	3r
3. (Wei⁴) hsiao¹- lang² i¹ ch'ü⁴ ching¹ chin¹ chiu³	7r
4. yü⁴ t'ai² pao³ chien⁴ sheng¹ ch'en²-kou⁴	7r
5. lü⁴ ch'uang¹ leng³-lo⁴ hsien² chen¹-hsiu⁴	7r
6. (ch'i³ chih¹ jen²) yü⁴ wan⁴ ch'uan⁴-erh² sung¹	5
7 (ch'i³ chih¹ jen²) liang³ yeh⁴ mei²-erh² chou⁴	5r

48C: *Word by word*

1. Why/worry?
2. Why/sad?
3. My man/once/left/till/today/long(time).
4. Jade/desk/precious/mirror/gathers/dust.
5. Green/window/cold and desolate/idle/needle/embroidery.
6. How/know/jade/wrist/bracelet/becomes loose.
7. How/know/two/leaf/eyebrows/knit?

48C: *First draft*

Why am I worried?
Why am I sad?
My husband has been gone too long.
The precious mirror on the jade desk has grown dust.
The green window is melancholy, and my embroidery needle is idle.
How would you know that the bracelet on my jade wrist has become loose?
How would you know that my two leaf-like eyebrows are knitted together?

POEM 48D: *Transliterated*

Tune: 'Shang⁴-ching¹-ma³'

1. t'a¹ ho²-ch'u⁴	3
2. kung⁴ shei² jen² hsieh²-shou³	5r

    3. hsiao³ ko² yin² p'ing² chih⁴ ko¹ chiu³   7r
    4. tsao³ wang⁴-liao³ chou⁴   4r
    5. pu¹ chi⁴-te² ti¹-ti¹ jou⁴   6r

48D: *Word by word*

1. He/where?
2. Together(with)/whom/hold/hands?
3. Small/tower/silver/screen/hesitant/songs/wine.
4. Already/forgot/oath(curse).
5. Not/remember/low-low/whisper.

48D: *First draft*

Where is he now?
With whom is he holding hands together?
In the small tower, behind the silver screen, songs and wine are spent.
I have forgotten the cursing.
I no longer remember the low whispers.

POEM 48E: *Transliterated*

Tune: 'Hou⁴-t'ing²-jua¹-sha⁴'

    1. yen³ hsiu⁴ an⁴ han² hsiu¹   5r
    2. k'ai¹ tsun¹ yüeh⁴ jang³ ch'ou²   5r
    3. men⁴ pa³ t'ai¹ ch'iang² hua⁴   5
    4. yung¹ chiang¹ chin³ tzu⁴ hsiu¹   5r
    5. tsui⁴ feng¹-liu²   3r
    6. chen¹-chen¹ en¹-ai⁴   4
    7. teng³-hsien² fen¹-fu⁴ teng³-hsien² hsiu¹   7r

48E. *Word by word*

1. Cover/sleeves/secretly/contain/bashfulness.
2. Open/jug/more/brew/sadness.
3. Depressed/get/mossy/walls/draw(paint).
4. Lazily/to have/silk/characters/study.
5. Most/romantic,
6. Truly/true/love(grace),
7. Idle/ordered(given)/idle/stop(finish).

48E: *First draft*

Covered with my sleeves I am secretly bashful.
Open the wine jug, more sadness is being brewed.
So depressed that I paint the mossy walls.
So lazy that I don't study the silk characters.
Indeed romantic
Is true love and true passion.
If it is given casually, it will cease casually.

SONG CHAIN II

Author: Po P'u
Mode: Hsien¹-lü³

POEM 49A: *Transliterated*

Tune: 'Tien³-chiang⁴-ch'un²'

1. chin¹ feng⁴ chai¹ fen²	4
2. yü⁴-ching¹-jen² ch'ü⁴	4
3. ch'iu¹ hsiao¹-sa³	3r
4. wan³ lai² hsien²-hsia²	4r
5. chen¹-hsien⁴ shou¹-shih² pa⁴	5r
6. tu² i³ wei¹-lou²	4
7. shih² erh⁴ chu¹-lien² kua⁴	5r
8. feng¹ hsiao¹-sa³	3r
9. yü³ ch'ing² yun² cha⁴	4r
10. chi² mu⁴ shan¹ ju² hua⁴	5r

49A: *Word by word*

1. Gold/hairpins/separated.
2. Jade/capital/person/gone.
3. Autumn/carefree(romantic).
4. Evening/came/idle(leisure).
5. Needle/thread/put away/finish.
6. Alone/lean/dangerous/tower.
7. Twelve/pearl/screen/hanging.
8. Wind/brisk/cold.
9. Rain/clears/clouds/over.
10. Exhaust/eyes/mountains/like/painting.

49A: *First draft*

My gold phoenix hairpins are being separated.
The man from the jade capital has left.
Autumn is so beautiful.
At evening I am idle.
The needle and thread have been put away.
I lean against the dangerous tower alone,
Hanging up the twelve pearl screen.
The wind blows briskly.
The rain is just over, clouds dispersed.
Straining my sight, the mountains look like a painting.

POEM 49B: *Transliterated*

Tune: 'Hun²-chiang¹-lung²'

1. tuan⁴ jen² ch'ang² ch'u⁴   4
2. t'ien¹ pien¹ ts'an²-chao⁴ shui³ pien¹ hsia²   7r
3. k'u¹ ho² su⁴ wu⁴   4
4. yüan³ shu⁴ ch'i¹ ya¹   4r
5. pai⁴ yeh⁴ fen¹-fen¹ yung¹ ch'i⁴ shih²   7
6. hsiu¹-chu² shan¹-shan¹ sao³ ch'uang¹-sha¹   7r
7. huang²-hun¹ chin⁴   3
8. ch'ou² sheng¹ chen¹ ch'u³   4
9. yüan⁴ ju⁴ p'i²-pa¹   4r

49B: *Word by word*

1. Break/person's/heart/place,
2. Heaven's/edge/remaining/sunset/water/edge/clouds.
3. Withered/lotus/sleeping/goose,
4. Distant/trees/perching/crows.
5. Fallen/leaves/numerous(plentiful)/holding/cut/rocks.
6. Cultivated/bamboos/gracefully/sweep/window's/silk.
7. Evening/nears.
8. Sadness/grows/mortar/pestle.
9. Complaint/enters/p'ipa.

49B: *First draft*

The places that break one's heart are
the remaining sunset at the edge of the sky and the colourful clouds at the edge of the river,
By the withered lotus, a sleeping goose,
On a distant tree, a perching crow.
The fallen leaves are embracing the cut rocks;
And the cultivated bamboos are touching the silk of the window.
The evening is close.
My sadness grows with the noise of the mortar sound.
And laments enter into my lute.

POEM 49C: *Transliterated*

Tune: 'Ch'uan¹-ch'uang¹-yüeh⁴'

1. i⁴ shu¹-k'uang² tsu³-ko¹ t'ien¹-ya²   7r
2. tsen³ chih¹ jen² mai²-yüan⁴ t'a¹   6r
3. yin² pien¹ tsui⁴ tao³ ch'ing¹-ts'ung¹ ma³   7r
4. (mo⁴ ch'ih¹) Ch'in²-lou² chiu³   3
5. Hsieh⁴-chia¹ ch'a²   3r
6. pu¹ ssu¹-liang⁴ chih¹ shou³ Lin²-ch'i¹ hua⁴   8r

49C: *Word by word*

1. Recall/undisciplined/crazy/separated/heaven's/edge.
2. How would/know/someone/blame/him?
3. Singing/whip/drunk/shaky/green/smart/horse.
4. Don't/eat Green/tower's/wine,
5. Hsieh/family's/tea.
6. Not/think/hold/hands/Lin-ch'i/words?

49C: *First draft*

I think of that undisciplined and crazy man separated by heaven's edge.
How would he know that someone is blaming him?
With his singing whip, he is drunk on his green, smart horse.
Don't drink wine at the green tower,
Or tea of the Hsieh family.
Don't you remember the words at Lin-ch'i while we held our hands?

POEM 49D: *Transliterated*

Tune: 'Chi^4-sheng^1-ts'ao^3'

1. p'ing² lan² chiu³	3
2. kui¹ hsiu⁴-ta²	3r
3. hsia⁴ wei¹-lou² ch'iang³ pa³ chin¹-lien² sa¹	8r
4. shen¹-ch'en² yüan⁴-yü³ chu¹-fei¹ ya³	7r
5. li⁴ ts'ang¹ t'ai² leng³ t'ou⁴ ling²-p'o¹-wa⁴	8r
6. shu³ kui¹-ch'i¹ k'ung¹ hua⁴ tuan³ ch'iung² tsan¹	8
7. wen¹ t'i² hen² p'in² shih¹ hsiang¹ lo² p'a⁴	8r

49D: *Word by word*

1. Lean on/banisters/long,
2. Return/embroidered/boudoir
3. Coming down/dangerous/tower/managed/to have/gold/lotus/loose.
4. Deep/courtyard/red/gate/silent.
5. Stand/mossy/terrace/cold/penetrates/thin/stockings.
6. Count/returning days/vainly/paint/short/jade/hairpin.
7. Wipe/weeping/marks/often/wet/fragrant/silk/kerchief.

49D: *First draft*

After leaning on the banisters too long,
I return to my embroidered boudoir.
Coming down the dangerous tower, I have to loosen my tiny shoes.
The tiny courtyard is deep and the red gate is quiet.
I stand on the mossy steps, and cold penetrates my thin stockings.
Counting his returning days, I paint with my short jade hairpin.
Wiping my tear marks, I often wet the fragrant silk kerchief.

POEM 49E: *Transliterated*

Tune: 'Yüan²-ho²-ling⁴'

1. i¹ ts'ung² chüeh² yen⁴-shu¹   5
2. chi³-tu⁴ chieh² kui¹-kua⁴   5r
3. ts'ui⁴ mei² ch'ang²-shih⁴ so³ li²-ch'ou² 7
4. yü⁴-jung² ch'iao²-ts'ui⁴ sha⁴   5r
5. tzu⁴ yüan²-hsiao¹ teng³-tai⁴ kuo⁴ ch'ung²-yang² 8
6. shen⁴ yu²-jan² pu¹ tao⁴ chia¹   6r

49E: *Word by word*

1. Once/since/cut off/goose/letters,
2. Several/times/tie(knot)/tortoise/divination.
3. Green/eyebrows/always/locked/departing/sorrow.
4. Jade/face/pale/greatly.
5. Since/Yüan-hsiao(festival)/wait/to pass/Ch'ung-yang(festival)
6. Indeed/still/not/arrive/home.

49E: *First draft*

Ever since the geese-sent letters were cut off,
I have consulted several times, with the tortoise divinations.
My green eyebrows are always locked in departing sorrow.
And my jade face has become pale.
Since the Yüan-hsiao I have waited till the Ch'ung-yang,
Still he has not come home yet.

POEM 49F: *Transliterated*

Tune: 'Shang⁴-ma³-chiao¹-sha⁴'

1. huan¹-hui⁴ shao³   3
2. fan²-nao³ to¹   3
3. hsin¹-hsü⁴ luan⁴ ju² ma²   5r
4. ou³-jan² hsing² chih⁴ tung¹ li² hsia⁴ 7r
5. tzu¹ chüeh² tzu¹ ya⁴   4r
6. leng³ ch'ing¹-ch'ing¹ ho² yüeh⁴ tui⁴ huang²-hua¹ 8r

49F: *Word by word*

1. Happy/meetings(gatherings)/few.
2. Sorrow/much.
3. Feelings/confused/as/hemp.
4. Accidentally/walk/to/eastern/fence/below.
5. Self/lament/self/sigh.
6. Cold/clearly/with/moon/face/yellow/flower.

49F: *First draft*

Our happy meetings are so few,
Yet my sorrow is so much.
My feelings are as confused as a bundle of hemp.
By accident, I walk to the foot of the east fence.
I lament and sigh alone.
I feel so cold facing the moon and the yellow flower.

SONG CHAIN III

Author: Ma Chih-yüan
Title: 'Ch'iu¹ ssu²'
Mode: Shuang¹-tiao⁴

POEM 50A: *Transliterated*

Tune: 'Yeh⁴-hsing²-ch'uan²'

1. pai³-sui⁴ kuang¹-yin¹ i¹ meng⁴ tieh⁴   7r
2. ch'ung² hui²-shou³ wang³-shih⁴ k'an¹ chüeh²   7r
3. chin¹-jih⁴ ch'un¹ lai²   4
4. ming²-chao¹ hua¹ hsieh⁴   4r
5. chi² fa² chan⁴ yeh⁴ lan² teng¹ mieh⁴   7r

50A: *Word by word*

1. (a)Hundred/years/time/one/dream(of)/butterfly.
2. Again/turn/head/past/events/can be/lamented.
3. Today/spring/comes.
4. Tomorrow/flowers/wither away.
5. Hurriedly/punish/cups/night/deep/lamp/put out.

50A: *First draft*

A hundred years of time are as but a butterfly's dream.
When I turn my head again, things of the past can be lamented.
Today spring comes.
Tomorrow flowers wither away.
Hurriedly I hold the wine cup, but night is deep, and my lamp is out.

POEM 50B: *Transliterated*

Tune: 'Ch'iao²-mu⁴-cha¹'

1. hsiang³ Ch'in²-kung¹ Han⁴-ch'üeh⁴   5r
2. (tou¹ tso⁴ liao³) shuai¹ ts'ao³ niu² yang² yeh³ 5r

133

3. (pu⁴ nin²-mo¹)　　　　　　　　　　　3
4. yü² ch'iao² mei² hua⁴ shuo¹　　　　　5r
5. tsung⁴ huang¹ fen²　　　　　　　　　3
6. heng² tuan⁴ pei¹　　　　　　　　　　3
7. pu¹ pien⁴ lung² she²　　　　　　　　4r

50B: *Word by word*

1. Think/Ch'in/palaces/Han/palaces,
2. All/became/withered/grass/cows/sheep/fields.
3. No/wonder/
4. Fisherman/woodsman/have no/words/to say.
5. Vertically/wild/tombs,
6. Horizontally/broken/monuments.
7. Not/distinguish/dragons/snakes.

50B: *First draft*

Think of those palaces of the Ch'in and Han dynasties,
They are all become grazing fields for cows and sheep.
No wonder
The fishermen and woodsmen have nothing to talk about.
Here are wild tombs,
There are broken monuments.
They cannot distinguish the dragons from snakes.

POEM 50C: *Transliterated*

Tune: 'Ch'ing⁴-Hsüan²-ho²'

1. t'ou² chih⁴ hu²-tsung¹ yü³ t'u⁴-hsüeh⁴　　7r
2. to¹-shao³ hao²-chieh²　　　　　　　　　　4r
3. ting³ tsu² sui¹ chien¹ pan⁴ yao¹ che¹　　　7r
4. Wei⁴ yeh² Chin⁴ yeh²　　　　　　　　　　4r

50C: *Word by word*

1. Thrown/into/fox/paths/and/hare/caves,
2. How many/heroes?
3. Tripod/feet/though/strong(firm)/half/waist/broken.
4. Wei/(or)Chin?

50C: *First draft*

Thrown into the caves of foxes and hares
Were how many heroes?
Though the feet of a tripod are strong, its waist is half broken.
Could it be Wei or Chin?

POEM 50D: *Transliterated*

Tune: 'Lo⁴ mei² feng¹'

1. t'ien¹ chiao⁴ (ni³) fu⁴   3
2. mo⁴ t'ai⁴ she¹   3r
3. mei² to¹ shih² hao³-t'ien¹ liang²-yeh⁴   7r
4. fu⁴-chia¹-erh²   3
5. keng⁴ tso⁴ tao⁴ (ni³) hsin¹ ssu⁴ t'ieh³   6r
6. cheng¹ ku¹-fu⁴ (liao³) chin³-t'ang² feng¹-yüeh⁴   7r

50D: *Word by word*

1. Heaven/makes/rich,
2. Don't be/too/extravagant.
3. Without/much/time/good/days/nice/nights.
4. Rich/family's/sons,
5. More/become/your/hearts/like/iron.
6. How/missed/painted/halls/wind/moon.

50D: *First draft*

If Heaven makes you rich,
Do not be too extravagant.
For not long are good days and nice nights.
The sons of a rich family,
Do not make your hearts like a piece of iron.
How you have missed the romance in the painted halls!

POEM 50E: *Transliterated*

Tune: 'Feng¹-ju⁴-sung¹'

1. yen³ ch'ien² hung² jih⁴ yu⁴ hsi¹ hsieh²   7r
2. chi¹ ssu⁴ hsia⁴ p'o¹ che¹   5r
3. pu¹-cheng¹ ching⁴-li³ t'ien¹ pai²-hsüeh³   7r
4. shang⁴ ch'uang² yü³ hsieh²-lü³ hsiang¹ pieh²   7r
5. hsiu¹ hsiao⁴ ch'ao² chiu¹ chi⁴-cho¹   6
6. hu²-lu²-t'i² i¹-hsiang⁴ chuang¹ tai¹   7r

50E: *Word by word*

1. Eyes/front/red/sun/again/west/slant.
2. Quick/as/down/slope/carriage.
3. Not/fight/mirror/inside/add/white/snow.
4. Go to/bed/with/shoes/mutual/separate.
5. Don't/laugh/nest/owls/scheme(plot)/clumsy.
6. Muddled/hitherto(so far)/pretend/dumb.

50E: *First draft*

Before my eyes, the red sun is slanting westward again,
Fast as a carriage going down hill.
How can one help it that in the mirror snow-white hair has been added.
Going to bed, one must separate with his shoes.
Don't laugh at the owl's lack of skill in making its nest.
Muddled, I have been pretending to be dumb.

POEM 50F: *Transliterated*

Tune: 'Po¹-pu¹-tuan⁴'

1. li⁴ ming² chieh⁴   3r
2. shih⁴-fei¹ chüeh²   3r
3. hung²-ch'en² pu¹ hsiang⁴ men² ch'ien² je³   7r
4. lü⁴ shu⁴ p'ien¹ i² wu¹ chiao³ che¹   7r
5. ch'ing¹ shan¹ cheng⁴ pu³ ch'iang² t'ou² ch'üeh¹   7r
6. (keng⁴ na³ k'an¹) chu²-li² mao²-she³   4r

50F: *Word by word*

1. Profit/name/cut off.
2. Right/wrong/finished.
3. Red/dust/not/toward/gate/front/aroused(stirred).
4. Green/tree/just/fit/room/corner/cover.
5. Blue/mountains/rightly/fill up/wall/top/crack.
6. Moreover/how/bear/bamboo/fence/grass/hut.

50F: *First draft*

Profit and fame are exhausted.
Right and wrong are cut off.
Red dust is no longer stirred up in front of my gate.
Green trees are fitting to cover the corner of the room.
Blue mountains are filling so well the cracks on the wall.
Besides, there are bamboo fences and a grass hut.

POEM 50G: *Transliterated*

Tune: 'Li²-t'ing²-yen⁴ tai⁴ Hsieh¹-chih³-sha⁴'

1. chu⁴ yin²-pa⁴ i¹-chiao⁴ ts'ai² ning²-t'ieh¹   8r
2. chi¹ ming² shih² wan⁴-shih¹ wu² hsiu¹-hsieh¹   8r
3. ho² nien² shih⁴ ch'e⁴   4r
4. (k'an³) mi⁴ tsa⁴-tsa⁴ i³ p'ai²-ping¹   6
5. luan⁴ fen¹-fen¹ feng¹ jang³ mi⁴   6
6. chi² jang³-jang³ ying² cheng¹ hsüeh³   6r
7. P'ei²-kung¹ Lü⁴-yeh³-t'ang²   5

8.	T'ao²-ling⁴ Pai²-lien²-she⁴	5r
9.	(ai⁴) ch'iu¹ lai² shih² na⁴-hsieh¹	5r
10.	ho² lu³ chai¹ huang²-hua¹	5
11.	tai⁴ shuang¹ fen¹ tzu³ hsieh⁴	5r
12.	chu³ chiu³ shao¹ hung² yeh⁴	5r
13.	hsiang³ jen²-sheng¹ yu³-hsien⁴ pei¹	6
14.	hun⁴ chi³-ke⁴ Ch'ung²-yang²-chieh²	6r
15.	jen² wen⁴ wo³ wan²-t'ung² chi⁴-che³	7r
16.	pien⁴ Pei³-hai³ t'an⁴ wu² lai³	6
17.	tao⁴ Tung¹-li² tsui⁴-liao³ yeh³	6r

50G: *Word by word*

1. Cricket/chirps/through/one/sleep/just/peaceful/comfortable.
2. Rooster/crows/time/ten thousand/things/no/stop.
3. What/year/is/end?
4. Look/crowdedly/ants/arrange/fights(battle),
5. Chaotically/bees/brew/honey,
6. Desperately/flies/fight for/blood.
7. Lord P'ei's/Green/Field/Hall.
8. Magistrate T'ao's/White/Lotus/Club.
9. Love/autumn/comes/time/those(things):
10. With/frost(dew)/pluck/yellow/flowers.
11. With/frost/divide/purple/crabs.
12. Warm/wine/burn/red/leaves.
13. Think/man's/life/limited/cup.
14. Manage/how many/Ch'ung-yang/festival?
15. Man/asks/me/(my) lad/remember:
16. Even/Pei-hai/visits/me/come,
17. Say/Tung-li/has drunk.

50G: *First draft*

After the cricket had finished chirping, I could then sleep in peace and comfort.
When the rooster crows again, ten thousand things will not stop.
When does this come to an end?
Look! crowding, the ants are arranging for a fight.
In chaos, the bees are busily brewing honey.
Desperately flies are fighting for blood.
In Lord P'ei's Green Field Hall,
Or Magistrate T'ao's White Lotus Club,
I love those things when autumn comes:
Mixed with dew pluck the yellow flowers.
In frost divide those purple crabs,
Warm wine by burning red leaves.
Think of the limited cup of a man's life,
How many Autumn festivals can he manage to enjoy?

If people ask about me, remember, my lad:
Even Pei-hai comes to visit me,
Tell him that Tung-li has already drunk.

50A–50G: *Notes*

Dreams of butterflies alludes to a story concerning the great Taoist philosopher Chuang-tzu who once dreamed that he had become a butterfly. Upon awaking he became perplexed by the question of whether, as a man, he had indeed dreamed that he was a butterfly, or whether, as a butterfly, he was indeed merely dreaming that he was a man.

Wei and Chin were two of the shortest lived dynasties in all of Chinese history.

Lord P'ei, or P'ei Tu of the T'ang dynasty, upon retiring, built himself a villa at the Noon Bridge, which he named 'Green Field Hall'.

T'ao was for a time during the Chin dynasty a local magistrate. He resigned and went into retirement.

Pei-hai refers to K'ung Jung of the late Han period. K'ung was well known for his hospitality. It is said that 'In his house, the guests were usually full: his wine jugs never empty'.

Tung-li is the courtesy name of Ma Chih-yüan, author of this 'chain'. The last two lines of this poem translate literally: 'When even a man as hospitable as K'ung Jung comes to visit me bringing wine, tell him that I am already well drunk'.

REMARKS ON THE TRANSLITERATED AND WORD-BY-WORD TEXTS

A. The Wade–Giles System of Transliteration.[*]

I. Initials and consonants:

ch	as j in Jack
ch'	as ch in chap
f	as f in fall
h	as h in hot
hs(i)	as sh in sheen
j	as *j* in French 'Je suis'
k	as g in got
k'	as k in kind
l	as l in lark
m	as m in mark
n	as n in not
p	as b in boat
p'	as p in pot
s	as s in sock
sh	as sh in Shaw
t	as d in dull
t'	as t in tot
ts	as z in zoo
ts'	as ts in catsup

II. Syllables for which no exact English equivalent can be found, i.e. these equivalents are only very roughly approximate:

Chih	as voiced dg sound in judge
ch'ih	as voiced ch in lurch
jih	as voiced ge in rouge
shih	as sh in mesh
tzu	as voiced z in buzz
tz'u	as ts in cats

III. Initial consonants that can also be used as medials or finals:

y	as y in yard, or medially written as *i* and pronounced as *ee* in feed
yü	umlaut ü as in German 'München', or, medially, written as *ü*.
w	as w in way or as *oo* sound as in food. When used medially is written as u in romanic

[*] Sir Thomas Francis Wade (1818–95) in his *Syllabary* and Herbert Allen Giles (1845–1935) in his *Chinese–English Dictionary* have between them worked out the so-called Wade–Giles system of romanization which has become the standard one used by Western scholars, and is the one employed in this book. Section A of the present appendix gives a simplified version of the Wade–Giles material.

IV. Vowels and finals:
1. Basic vowels:*
   - a   as a in ah or far
   - e   as u in mud, only elongated.
   - eh   as e in yet
   - i   as ee in fee or see
   - o   as aw in law or a in malt
   - u   as oo in food
   - ü   umlaut u as in French 'une'
2. Diphthongs:
   - ai   as i in high
   - ao   as ou in ouch
   - ei   as a in hay
   - iu   as ew in new
   - ou   as ow in low
3. Vowels a and e in combination with n and ng:
   - an   as on in won
   - ang as ong in long
   - en   as un in begun
   - eng as ung in sung

V. Capitalization:

Capital letters are used only for proper names, personal or geographical. In Chinese names, the family (last) name always comes first, and the given name (first name) last. If the given name is only one character, it is capitalized. But if the given name is composed of two characters, then the first character is capitalized, and the second character is not, but the two characters are joined by a hyphen, as in the name Kuan Han-ch'ing, where Kuan indicates the family name, and Han-ch'ing is the given name. As for geographical names, such as the name of the Yüan capital, Ta-tu, the first character is capitalized and the second character is not; but the two are joined by a hyphen. The names of dynasties are always capitalized, such as Han, Yüan, etc.

VI. Tones

Tones in modern Chinese are as important as accents in modern English. These tones in Chinese actually amount to different pitches in pronunciation—which is to say that the same consonant-vowel combinations of sounds in Chinese are not always sounded according to the same tones. By way of indicating the major tones of modern Chinese we have used the numbers 1, 2, 3, 4 over each word to identify its tone.

* All vowels in Chinese are long vowels.

The first tone is level, with a high pitch. The second tone, called a rising tone, starts out low and rises, as with the word 'me' used in the English question, 'Who, *me?*' The third tone is a curving tone, so called because it starts by falling and then rises or curves up, as in the English utterance 'uh-huh' when used to indicate agreement in conversation. The fourth tone, or falling tone, is so called because it starts at a given level, descends, and finally drops—as when a person is heaving a deep sigh. Although these tones are important features of the Chinese language, they do not in poetry affect the rhyming of words or characters. We have accordingly indicated tones primarily for the benefit of students of the Chinese language.

B. 'Cuttings'

In the word-by-word translations presented in the appendices to each poem, the literal meaning of each Chinese character is separated from that of each following character by a slant line, or 'cutting'. Thus:

since/send/separated stands for the three characters: *tzu/sung/pieh.*

Originally, written Chinese was almost exclusively monosyllabic. However, since even monosyllables, representing words and ideas, inevitably become rich in nuances, it has become necessary for us in many cases to suggest alternative translation words, given in parentheses, immediately following each primary translation word. Thus in:

a (one)/ point (bit)/ mutual/ thinking (longing) etc.

the words (one) (bit) (longing) are alternative translation words for the characters indicated as meaning *a, point, thinking.*

But the Yüan Chinese poets were making ever increasing use of polysyllabic–colloquial constructions. These colloquial meanings, which supplement, but have not usually superseded the original meanings of the basic individual characters as words, are indicated in brackets. In each case the bracketed words give the meaning corresponding to the two (in rare cases three) preceding characters taken altogether. For example in:

since/send/separated [leave-taking or departure]

'send' gives the basic meaning of the character *sung*; 'separated' provides the basic idea of the character *pieh*, as shown by the phrase in brackets, both of these ideas, of 'to send off', or 'to send away', *and* 'to separate', taken together combine to result in the colloquial bisyllabic word *sung/pieh*, which suggests leave-taking, departure, saying good-bye.

During the time of Yüan, compound words, namely words made up of two characters, were quite common. For cutting purpose, we consider such compounds as words, not as two characters; for example, yu-fu/ meaning fisherman; yuan-yang/ meaning mandarin ducks (always a pair); ying-hsiung/ meaning heroes; ch'ou-ch'u/ meaning wandering.

BIOGRAPHICAL SKETCHES

(Note: The reference numbers correspond to the *Index of Poets* on Page ooo)

(1) Anonymous.

(2) Nothing is known of Ch'a Te-ch'ing.

(3) Chang K'e-chiu, also known as Hsiao-shan, came from Ch'ing-yüan (presently Chekiang Province).

(4) Chang Yang-hao, also known as Yun-chuang, took the courtesy name of Hsi-meng. Originally from Chi-nan (presently Shantung Province), he served as Minister of Rites at the Yüan court. Disagreeing with the policies of the government, he resigned from public service and retired to his native home. Later, during the second year of the T'ien-li reign of the Emperor Wen-tsung (AD 1331), the central area of the Yellow River valley being plagued by drought, Chang Yang-hao accepted appointment as special commissioner in charge of relief in the drought area. He not only donated most of his personal wealth in order to aid the distressed in this district, but appears in addition to have worked himself to death in their cause. Chang's *ch'ü* have been collected in a volume entitled *Yun-chuang yüeh-fu* (*Ballads of Yun-chuang*). Chang's biography is included in the *Yüan shih, chüan* 175.

(5) Ch'iao Chi also known as Chi-fu (his courtesy name Meng-fu), was a native of T'ai-yuan (presently Shansi Province). He lived for many years in Hangchow (presently in Chekiang Province). He was known for his handsome appearance. Being very strict with himself, people respected him very much. He wrote an operatic play entitled *Yang-chow meng* (*Dream in Yangchow*) that gained him outstanding recognition as a playwright. His songs were compiled into two volumes, one titled *Ch'iao Meng-fu hsiao-ling*, the other *Meng-fu san-ch'ü*. Many of these songs are still available today and are included in the collection entitled *San-ch'ü ts'ung-k'an*. Ch'iao died in the fifth year of the reign Chih-cheng of Emperor Shun-ti (AD 1345).

(6) Chung Ssu-ch'eng, courtesy name Chi-hsien, was so ugly that he was given the studio name Ch'ou-chai (Studio of Ugliness). A native of Honan, he lived at Hanchow most of his life. He wrote the famous *Lu kui pu* (*Record of Ghosts*) in which the names of the known Yüan dramatists and their works are listed. Although he is believed to have lived during the late Yüan and early Ming periods, his exact dates are not known.

(7) Hsü Tsai-ssu, also known as Te-k'e, came from Chia-hsing (presently in Chekiang Province). He served for a time as a clerk for the local road administration. He was so fond of sweets that he was given the name, T'ien-chai (Studio of Sweets). His dates are unknown.

(8) Nothing is known of Hsüeh Ang-fu.

(9) Hu Chih-yü was a native of what is now Hopei Province. He was

also known as Shao-k'ai. His *ch'ü* are available in a collection entitled *Tzu-shan ta-ch'üan-chi*. He was born in the fourth year of the reign of the Emperor Ai-tsung of Chin (AD 1228) and died in the thirtieth year of the reign of the Emperor Shih-tsu of Yüan (AD 1290).

(10) Jen Yü, courtesy name Tse-ming, was a native of Ssu-ming (currently Chekiang Province). He probably wrote during the latter part of the Yüan.

(11) Kuan Han-ch'ing lived in Ta-tu (presently Peking), capitol of Yüan. His studio name was I-chai-sou. For a time a clerk at the Royal Hospital, he devoted his literary efforts to writing *ch'ü* and operatic drama. In his songs, or *ch'ü*, Kuan wrote mostly on romantic topics. Although he is known to have written more than sixty operatic plays, only fourteen have been preserved. The critic Chung Ssu-ch'eng, writing near the end of the Yüan period, in his *Lu kui pu, Records of Ghosts* (i.e. *Prominent Playwrights of Yüan Drama*), judged Kuan the best.

(12) Kuan Yun-shih, originally named Hsiao-yun-shih-hai-ya, was an assimilated Moslem. His grandfather, Ali-haiya, having aided the Mongols in conquering the Sung dynasty, was rewarded with the title of Prince of the State of Ch'u. Hsiao, in recognition of his father, Kuan-chih-ko, took the surname Kuan. Inheriting his father's position as *Ta-lu-hua-ch'ih* (or head) of the two Huai districts, he later gave up the title to his brother and became a student of Yao Sui. During the reign of the Emperor Jen-tsung (AD 1312–21) Kuan became advisor to the Han-lin Academy.

(13) Nothing is known of Li Chih-yüan.

(14) Liu Chih, also known as Shih-chung, came from what is presently Shensi Province. He served in various positions for the Yüan government and was known as an official of decency and integrity. Chung Ssu-ch'eng, author of *Lu kui pu*, lists Liu as 'one of the famous men of the present time'. Liu was approximately contemporary with Chung, who lived during the later Yüan period. Chung was born during the seventeenth year of the Chih-yüan of the Emperor Shih-tsu (AD 1281).

(15) Lu Chih, also known as Hsin-lao, took the courtesy name of Ch'u-tao. He came originally from Cho-chun (currently Hopei Province). Lu received his *chin-shih* degree during the fifth year of the reign of Chih-yuan (AD 1269). He served as Chief Administrator of the Route of Honan, as Censor of the Chiang-tung Circuit, and as Advisor to the Emperor. Lu was known both for his poetry and for his essays. He was born in the seventh year of the reign of the Emperor T'ai-tsung (AD 1236), and died in the fourth year of the Ta-te reign of the Emperor Ch'eng-tsung (AD 1306).

(16) Ma Chih-yüan, whose courtesy name was Tung-li, was a native of Ta-tu, capitol of Yüan. He served as administrative officer in the

provincial government of Chiang-che Province. He wrote many *ch'ü* and a number of operatic plays. The critic Chu Ch'üan, writing in *T'ai-ho cheng-yin-p'u* (*Study of Prosody*), during the early part of the Ming dynasty, praised Ma Chih-yüan as the foremost playwright of the Yüan period, characterizing Ma's plays as similar to the 'Chirping phoenix in the morning sun'. Ma was probably born early in the reign of the Emperor Shih-tsu of Yüan (*c.* AD 1260), and probably died near the end of the Yüan (*c.* AD 1341). As a dramatist, Ma wrote plays involving mostly religious, i.e. Taoist, themes.

(17) Ma Chiu-kao, also known as Ang-fu, was an assimilated Moslem. He served as Supervisor of the T'ai-p'ing Circuit and was recognized as an especially fine calligrapher.

(18) Pai Pen, also known as Wu-chiu, was a native of Ch'ien-t'ang, in what is presently Chekiang Province. He is mentioned in Chung Ssu-ch'eng's *Lu kui pu* (*Record of Ghosts*) as 'one of the previous generation'.

(19) Po P'u, also known as Jen-fu, was a native of Chen-ting, in what is now Hopei Province. Po's father Po Hua (courtesy name Wen-chü) had served as judge in the Privy Council of the Chin Court. With the fall of Chin, Po Hua retired from public life. His son, the poet Po P'u, was tutored in childhood by the famous Yüan scholar Yüan Hao-wen. Having become disillusioned by his service as a soldier and by the fall of Chin, Po P'u, declined to seek office under the new government, and chose instead to wander throughout the country. His opera titled, in English, *Rain on the Wu-t'ung Tree*, is considered one of the best of the period. Po P'u was born in the third year of the Cheng-ta reign of the Emperor Ai-tsung of Chin (AD 1227) and died after the twenty-eighth year of Chih-yüan in the reign of the Emperor Shih-tsu (AD 1291).

(20) Nothing is known of Sun Chou-ch'ing.

(21) Teng Yü-pin probably lived during the early period of the Yüan. No record of him appears to be extant.

(22) Wang Yun, also known as Chung-mou, came from what is presently Honan Province. Under the Yüan he was made a member of the Han-lin Academy. His collected works are entitled *Ch'iu-chien ta ch'üan chi*. He wrote more than forty *ch'ü* which appear in his collected works. He was born during the fourth year of the Cheng-ta reign of the Emperor Ai-tsung of Chin (AD 1228) and died in the eighth year of the Ta-te reign of the Emperor Ch'en-tsung of Yüan (AD 1306).

(23) Yang Kuo, also called Cheng-ch'ing, took the courtesy or pen-name of Hsi-an. A native of P'u-yin (in what is presently Hopei Province), Yang earned his *chin-shih* (the highest possible academic) degree during the first year of the Cheng-ta reign of the Emperor Ai-tsung of Chin (AD 1224). Under the Yüan, he served in the government as censor. He lived for seventy-five years. His biography is included in the *Yüan shih* or History of Yüan, *chüan* (i.e. volume) 146.

(24) Yao Sui, also known as Tuan-fu, took the courtesy name of Mu-an. He was known as a classicist. He served in various minor positions for the Yüan government. He was born in the tenth year of the reign of the Emperor T'ai-tsung of Yüan (AD 1239) and died in the second year of the Huang-ch'ing reign of the Emperor Jen-tsung of Yüan (AD 1313). His biography is included in the *Yüan shih, chüan* 174.

INDEX OF POETS, AND POEM NUMBERS

(1) Anonymous, 14, 15, 45
(2) Ch'a Te-ch'ing, 30
(3) Chang K'e-chiu, 34, 35, 37, 38, 39, 40
(4) Chang Yang-hao, 12, 13, 16
(5) Ch'iao Chi, 41, 42
(6) Chung Ssu-ch'eng, 47
(7) Hsü Tsai-ssu, 36
(8) Hsüeh Ang-fu, 22, 23
(9) Hu Chih-yü, 7, 8
(10) Jen Yü, 28, 29
(11) Kuan Han-ch'ing, 1, 48
(12) Kuan Yun-shih, 17, 44
(13) Li Chih-yüan, 24
(14) Liu Chih, 25
(15) Lu Chih, 31
(16) Ma Chih-yüan, 11, 20, 32, 33, 50
(17) Ma Chiu-kao, 26, 27
(18) Pai Pen, 19
(19) Po P'u, 2, 3, 4, 49
(20) Sun Chou-ch'ing, 46
(21) Teng Yü-pin, 18
(22) Wang Yun, 43
(23) Yang Kuo, 5, 6
(24) Yao Sui, 9, 10, 21

INDEX OF ENGLISH TITLES, AND POEM NUMBERS

'A New Life', 16
'Autumn', 50
'Autumn Dream', 39
'Autumnal Song', 7
'Career Song', 3
'Clearing Weather', 20
'Collating Ancient Verse', 27
'Consolatory Thought', 13
'Courtesan's Song', 46
'Drink Song', 2
'Evening Scene', 43
'Fond Farewell', 25
'Grave Heroes', 14
'Harmonizing with a Friend's Rhyme', 28
'Heroes of the Past', 30
'Homecoming', 32
'Landscape', 31
'Late Spring Song of a Wife', 24
'Leisure Living', 18
'Lotus Song, I', 5
'Lotus Song, II', 6
'Lying Low', 29
'Meditation in Autumn', 11
'Nonconformist', 36
'Old Fisherman's Song', 4
'Old Man's Spring Song' I, 22
'Old Man's Spring Song' II, 23
'Old Scholar's Spring Song', 10
'Old Soldier's Song', 15
'On Visiting Prince Yueh-fu's Estate', 41
'Pastoral Painter', 19
'Query', 33
'Renascence', 44
'Sad Courtesan', 45
'Sad Parting', 1
'Sad Question', 12
'Sad Spring Song', 47
'Sad Thoughts in Spring', 38
'Sad Wives and Courtesans', 49
'Sadness in Spring', 34
'Song for the Seasons', 21
'Spring Night', 37
'Spring Song', 8
'Tears from the Boudoir', 48
'The Ruins of Yüeh', 42

'Thinking in Autumn', 40
'Thinking of the Past at Ling-chiao's
    Tower', 26
'Thoughts in Autumn', 35
'Winter Song', 9
'Written for Someone', 17

INDEX OF FIRST LINES, AND POEM NUMBERS

As sun shines, 20
As warm winds excite, 25
Awake from, 34
Beautiful mountains and, 29
At Parrot Beach I live next, 19
Bearing fresh, 32
Before my eyes the sun slants, 50E
Centuries pass with dreams of, 50A
Chill West winds cause, 48B
Crickets cease chirping—I sleep. At, 50G
Despite west winds, come welcomed geese. 17
Discarding, 50F
Drink deep. What matters? Who, 2
Dry vine, tree, evening crow: 11
Employed by, 40
Fighting with, 15
Fishers and woodsmen, 50B
Fishing willowed stream, seining, 4
Fled from fierce merit and fame, 16
Flower-shaped mirrors crack. 38
Geese lace cold white clouds. Jade, 35
Gentle winds, 44
Grass grows green, 21
Grass huts fall before strong, 28
Happiness, 49F
Heaven-sent, 50D
I cannot, 1
I hide my face with, 48E
I remove my, 49A
I think of that crazy old, 49C
Idle for years, beside rivers, 27
Impeached, 13
King Pa was brave; he saved his, 14
Leisure loving old man, 36
Lotus leaves now fade—even as, 7
Lotus picking, I come late. 6
Midst ochre dust, by rice, 42
Mountain rains swell rivers. From, 48A
My brush fixes time with ink. 10
My heart breaks twice: 49B
Near these yellow hills once lived, 26
Past inebriates of, 22
Plum blossoms tell me Spring is, 47
Sad winds sough through empty courts. 45
Seeing the, 24
Should wives weep, 48C
Showered swings at sunset, this, 46
Sing! Pick lotus! Let orchid, 5
Sun and moon rotate. 18
Tear-spent grass, 3

Ten years of song 'neath moons, 9
Though tripods are strong, break one, 50C
Unable to retain, 23
Waiting too, 49D
Wearing plain, 33
West winds bring letters asking, 39
Who were our heroes? Fishers, 30
Wine-sick poet, midst blossoms, 37
With flute songs dreams now sink, 41
With light shirt and short hat I, 8
With whom does, 48D
Withered pines project from cliffs, 31
Who fathoms, 12
Words of lotus pickers mix, 43
You have not written. 49E

For Product Safety Concerns and Information please contact our EU
representative GPSR@taylorandfrancis.com
Taylor & Francis Verlag GmbH, Kaufingerstraße 24, 80331 München, Germany

www.ingramcontent.com/pod-product-compliance
Lightning Source LLC
Chambersburg PA
CBHW070622300426
44113CB00010B/1622